A RUMOR OF ANGELS

Peter L. Berger is University Professor at Boston University. His publications in the field of religion include *The Noise of Solemn Assemblies* and *The Precarious Vision*, both critical analyses of Protestant life and thought in America, *A Rumor of Angels: Modern Society and the Rediscovery of the Supernatural*, and *The Heretical Imperative: Contemporary Possibilities of Religious Affirmation*. He is the editor of *The Other Side of God: A Polarity in World Religions*. His best known book in sociology is *Invitation to Sociology*. The present volume develops further the novel approach to sociological theory proposed in *The Social Construction of Reality—A Treatise in the Sociology of Knowledge*, written in collaboration with Thomas Luckmann.

A RUMOR OF ANGELS

Modern Society and the Rediscovery of the Supernatural

Peter L. Berger

ANCHOR BOOKS

DOUBLEDAY & COMPANY, INC.

GARDEN CITY, N.Y.

*A Rumor of Angels: Modern Society
and the Rediscovery of the Supernatural*
was originally published in hardcover
by Doubleday & Company, Inc.

Anchor Books edition: 1970

BVG 01

TO THE MEMORY OF
FREDERICK NEUMANN
1899–1967

Contents

Preface

This book is concerned with the possibility of theological thinking in our present situation. It asks whether such thinking is possible at all today and, if so, in what way. The first question is answered affirmatively, and the answer is, up to a point, supported by an argument that derives from sociology. In the very tentative approaches made to an answer of the second question, sociology is of little if any use. It should, therefore, be very clear that I can claim no authority as a sociologist for a good deal of what follows here. This means that I'm sticking my neck out in the most blatant way, and I should probably explain my motives.

In a recent book, *The Sacred Canopy—Elements of a Sociological Theory of Religion* (Garden City, N.Y., Doubleday, 1967), I attempted to summarize what seem to me to be certain essential features of a sociological perspective on religion and I tried to apply this perspective to an analysis of the contemporary religious situation. I have been trained in a sociological tradition shaped by Max Weber and so I tried, to the best of my ability, to keep my statements "value-free." The result was a theoretical work that, quite apart from the technical jargon in which it had to be presented, read like a treatise on atheism, at least in parts. The analysis of the contemporary situation with which it ended could easily be read (and, as far as my intentions were concerned, misread) as a counsel of despair for religion in the modern world. For better or for worse, my self-understanding is not exhausted by the fact that I am a sociologist. I also consider myself a Christian, though I have not yet found the heresy into which my theological views would comfortably fit. All this made me uneasy about the possible effect of *The Sacred Canopy* upon the unwary reader and so I added an appendix that dealt with some possible theological implications of the book's argument. This way out did not satisfy me, and the present book is the result of this dissatisfaction.

In what follows I try to say what I have to say as simply as I can and without forcing the reader to go first through the conceptual and terminological apparatus with which I habitually carry on my business as a sociologist. I have found a few technical terms indispensable, but I have tried to keep these to a minimum. This book, then, is not particularly addressed to sociologists and does not presuppose the debatable benefits of a sociological education. It is addressed to anyone with a concern for religious questions and the willingness to think about them systematically. I hope that it may have something to say to theologians, though I'm fully aware of my lack of expertise in theology. In view of the non-technical (I'm tempted to say unprofessional) character of the book, I have also kept the notes to a minimum and almost entirely limited them to references in English. The relatively frequent references to previous writings of my own should in no way be construed as a conviction on my part that these writings are terribly important or as advice to the reader to go back to them. But every process of thinking must be a conversation with oneself and particularly with one's previous thought, and one cannot at each step start all over again from the beginning. Not to have to do this should perhaps be one of the fringe benefits of having written more than one book.

I suppose one sticks one's neck out when it comes to things one deems important. I think that religion is of very great importance at any time and of particular importance in our own time. If theologizing means simply any systematic reflection about religion, then it would seem plausible to regard it as too important to leave to the theological experts. Ergo, one must stick out one's neck. This implies impertinence as well as modesty. To try at all may well be impertinent. This should make it all the clearer that the effort is tentative and the result unfinished.

Some of the ideas that follow were discussed at length with Richard Neuhaus. I would like to express my great appreciation of his interest and suggestions on these occasions.

I have dedicated this book to my first teacher in theology. I know that he would not have liked many of its conclusions, but I venture to hope that he would have approved the basic intention.

P. L. B.

New York, Fall 1968

A RUMOR OF ANGELS

1. The Alleged Demise of the Supernatural

If commentators on the contemporary situation of religion agree about anything, it is that the supernatural has departed from the modern world. This departure may be stated in such dramatic formulations as "God is dead" or "the post-Christian era." Or it may be undramatically assumed as a global and probably irreversible trend. Thus the "radical theologian" Thomas Altizer tells us with the solemnity of a confessional pronouncement that "we must realize that the death of God is an historical event, that God has died in our cosmos, in our history, in our *Existenz*."[1] And Herman Kahn and Anthony Wiener, of the Hudson Institute, in their fascinating attempt to project the course of the final third of this century, manage to do so with only minimal mention of religion and on the assumption that twentieth-century cultures will continue to be increasingly "sensate"—a term coined by the late Harvard sociologist Pitirim Sorokin, and defined by Kahn and Wiener as "empirical, this-worldly, secular, humanistic, pragmatic, utilitarian, contractual, epicurean or hedonistic, and the like."[2]

The departure of the supernatural has been received in a variety of moods—with prophetic anger, in deep sorrow, with gleeful triumph, or simply as an emotionally unprovocative fact. But the spokesman of traditional religion who thunders against a godless age, the "progressive" intellectual who hails its coming, and the dispassionate analyst who merely registers it have in common the recognition that such, indeed, is our situation—an age in which the divine, at least in its classical forms, has receded into the background of human concern and consciousness.

The term "supernatural" has been justly criticized on a number of grounds. Historians of religion and cultural anthropologists have pointed out that the term suggests the division of reality into a closed system of rationally comprehensible "nature" and a mysterious world somehow beyond it, a peculiarly modern conception, which is misleading if one seeks to understand the religious notions of primitive or archaic cultures. Biblical scholars have criticized the term as failing to convey the concreteness and historical character of the Israelite religious experience, and Christian theologians attacked it as offending the world-affirming implications of the doctrine of the incarnation, if not indeed of the doctrine of creation. Nevertheless the term, particularly in its everyday usage, denotes a fundamental category of religion, namely the assertion or belief that there is *an other reality,* and one of ultimate significance for man, which transcends the reality within which our everyday experience unfolds. It is this fundamental assumption about reality, rather than this or that historical variation of it, that is allegedly defunct or in the process of becoming defunct in the modern world.

The historian of religion, Rudolf Otto, in *The Idea of the Holy* (originally published in German in 1917) attempted what may still be regarded as a definitive description of this "otherness" of religious experience. Otto emphasized that the sacred (that is, the reality man believes he encounters in religious experience) is "totally other" than ordinary, human phenomena, and in this "otherness" the sacred impresses man as an overwhelming, awesome, and strangely fascinating power.

As one might expect, there has been extensive controversy since then as to the validity of Otto's delineation of the sacred as the religious category par excellence in all cultures. Once more, however, these scholarly debates may be left aside. Instead, let us look at the ordinary world, which some philosophers have called the *Lebenswelt,* or "life-world," within which we carry on our "normal" activities in collaboration with other men. This is the arena of most of our projects in life, whose reality is strongest and thus the most "natural" in our consciousness. This, in the words of the social philosopher Alfred Schutz, is "the world of daily life which the wide-awake, grown-up man who acts in it and upon it amidst his fellow-man experiences within the natural attitude as a reality."[3] It is to this domain of taken-for-granted, "natural" experience (*not* necessarily to "nature" in the sense of, say, the eighteenth-century rationalists) that religion posits a "supernatural" reality.

As cultural anthropologists have pointed out, the everyday life of primitive man was, like ours, dominated by empirical, pragmatic, utilitarian imperatives geared to "this world"; he could hardly have solved the basic problems of survival if it had not been. This was even more true of daily life in the great ancient civilizations. The preoccupation with "natural" consciousness is not at all peculiar to the modern age. Someone once remarked that most present-day Anglo-American philosophers have the same conception of reality as that held by a slightly drowsy, middle-aged businessman right after lunch. Very probably slightly drowsy, middle-aged tribal warriors and ancient Greeks held very similar conceptions right after *their* lunches. But primitive and ancient men also accepted the idea of another, supernatural world of divine beings and forces as a background to the ordinary world and assumed that "the other world" impinged on this one in a variety of ways. This suggests that at least part of the reason why we today have embraced what we consider the "rationality" (or "naturalism") of modern science and philosophy is because we wish to maintain that "natural" consciousness is the only possible or desirable one—a point that will be taken up again later.

There is a German fairy tale about a young apprentice who is disturbed by the fact that he has never been able to experience gruesomeness and deliberately subjects himself to all sorts of situations that are reputed to evoke such feelings. The spiritual adventure of modern man seems to have been motivated by the opposite aim of *un*learning any conceivable metaphysical terror. If the idea about the demise of the supernatural is correct, then the unlearning effort has indeed succeeded. How much evidence is there in support of the idea?

The answer hinges on what might be called the secularization theory of modern culture—using the word secularization not in the sense of what has happened with social institutions (such as, for example, the separation of church and state), but as applying to processes inside the human mind, that is, a secularization of *consciousness*. Here the empirical evidence is not very satisfactory. Considering the importance of the question, one might have expected professional observers of the contemporary scene, especially sociologists, to invest some energy in an attempt to provide answers. But in recent years sociologists, with very few exceptions, have shown very little interest, probably because they have sworn allegiance to a scientific "progressivism" that regards religion as a vanishing leftover from the dark ages of superstition and do not care to invest their energies in the study of a moribund phenomenon. The fairly small group of sociologists who have taken the sociology of religion as their professional specialty have not been terribly helpful either.[4] They have not looked on religion as moribund, if only for reasons of professional self-respect, but they have regarded it almost exclusively in terms of the traditional religious institutions—that is, most recent sociology of religion has been a sociology *of the churches*. And it is from this somewhat restricted perspective that a good deal of sound evidence has, indeed, been accumulated on secularization. The largest body of data, most of which refer to Europe, comes from the school of so-called "religious sociology," which is largely Catholic-inspired.[5] Recently there have been some interesting attempts quite distinct from this school to uncover motives for religious participation in America with the use of more sophisticated research tools.[6]

On the basis of this evidence one can say with some confidence that *churchly* religiosity (that is, religious belief and practice within the traditions of the principal Christian churches) has been on the decline in modern society. In Europe this has generally taken the form of a progressive decline in institutional participation (attendance at worship, use of the sacraments, and the like), though there are important class differences in this. In America, on the contrary, there has been an increase in participation (as measured by church membership figures), though there are good reasons to think that the motives for participation have changed greatly from the traditional ones. It is safe to say that, compared to earlier historical periods, fewer Americans today adhere to the churches out of a burning desire for salvation from sin and hellfire, while many do so out of a desire to provide moral instruction for their children and direction for their family life, or just because it is part of the life style of their particular neighborhood. The difference between the European and American patterns has been aptly characterized by the sociologist Thomas Luckmann as, respectively, "secularization from without" and "secularization from within." In both cases there is strong evidence that traditional religious beliefs have become empty of meaning not only in large sections of the general population but even among many people who, with whatever motives, continue to belong to a church. All this, of course, leaves open the question of whether there may not be genuinely religious forces outside the traditional Christian or churchly frame of reference. Also, since sociologists and their ilk have been around for only a rather short time, it is not clear to what extent their findings can be rigorously compared with the situation in previous periods, for which different and only imperfectly comparable data are available. Sociologists, equipped with all the latest tricks of their trade, may be able to tell us with some precision why people join churches in America in the 1960s; to compare their findings with the situation in the 1860s we have to rely on what they would call much "softer" data.

All the same, the proposition of the demise of the supernatural, or at least of its considerable decline, in the modern world is very plausible in terms of the available evidence. It is to be hoped that more plentiful and more precise evidence will yet be produced, and that there will be greater collaboration between social scientists and historians in this undertaking. But even now we have as good an empirical foundation for the proposition as we do for most generalizations about our world. Whatever the situation may have been in the past, *today* the supernatural as a meaningful reality is absent or remote from the horizons of everyday life of large numbers, very probably of the majority, of people in modern societies, who seem to manage to get along without it quite well. This means that those to whom the supernatural is still, or again, a meaningful reality find themselves in the status of a minority, more precisely, a *cognitive minority*—a very important consequence with very far-reaching implications.

By a cognitive minority I mean a group of people whose view of the world differs significantly from the one generally taken for granted in their society. Put differently, a cognitive minority is a group formed around a body of deviant "knowledge." The quotation marks should be stressed here. The term "knowledge" used within the frame of reference of the sociology of knowledge always refers to what is *taken to be* or *believed as* "knowledge." In other words, the use of the terms is strictly neutral on the question of whether or not the socially held "knowledge" is finally true or false. All human societies are based on "knowledge" in this sense. The sociology of knowledge seeks to understand the different forms of this. The same quotation marks apply to my use of the adjective "cognitive," of course. Instead of saying that societies have bodies of knowledge, we can say that they have cognitive structures. Once more, this in no way implies a judgment of the final validity of these "cognitions." This should be kept in mind whenever the adjective is used in the following argument. Put simply, the sociologist qua sociologist always stays in the role of reporter. He reports that people believe they "know" such and such, and that this belief has such and such consequences. As soon as he ventures an opinion on whether the belief is finally justified, he is jumping out of the role of sociologist. There is nothing wrong with this role change, and I intend to perform it myself in a little while. But one should be clear about what one is doing when.

For better or for worse, men are social beings. Their "sociality" includes what they think, or believe they "know" about the world.[7] Most of what we "know" we have taken on the authority of others, and it is only as others continue to confirm this "knowledge" that it continues to be plausible to us. It is such socially shared, socially taken-for-granted "knowledge" that allows us to move with a measure of confidence through everyday life. Conversely, the plausibility of "knowledge" that is not socially shared, that is challenged by our fellow men, is imperiled, not just in our dealings with others, but much more importantly in our own minds. The status of a cognitive minority is thus invariably an uncomfortable one—not necessarily because the majority is repressive or intolerant, but simply because it refuses to accept the minority's definitions of reality *as* "knowledge." At best, a minority viewpoint is forced to be defensive. At worst, it ceases to be plausible to anyone.

Highly intriguing studies, which it would be unpractical to review here, have been made of this social dimension of our cognitive life.[8] One example may illustrate its importance. A person coming to America from a culture in which it is part of everyone's "knowledge" that the stars influence human events will, if he expresses this "knowledge" in the United States, soon discover what it means to belong to a cognitive minority. He will be listened to with shocked surprise or tolerant amusement. Attempts may be made to "educate" him, or he may be encouraged to exhibit his exotic notions and thus to play the role of ethnological specimen. Unless he can insulate himself against this massive challenge to his previously taken-for-granted reality (which would presuppose an available group of fellow astrologers to take refuge with), he will soon begin to doubt his challenged "knowledge." There are various ways of coping with doubt. Our cognitive exile could decide to keep his truths to himself —thus depriving them of all social support—or he could try to gain converts; or he could seek for some sort of compromise, perhaps by thinking up "scientific" reasons for the validity of his astrological lore, thus contaminating his reality with the cognitive assumptions of his challengers. Individuals vary in their ability to resist social pressure. The predictable conclusion of the unequal struggle is, however, the progressive disintegration of the plausibility of the challenged "knowledge" in the consciousness of the one holding it. The example may seem loaded—after all, presumably both the writer and the readers of this book "know" that astrology is a lot of nonsense.

To make the point clearer, the example can be reversed. An American stranded in an astrological culture will find his "scientific" view of the world tottering under exactly the same social assaults that undermine astrology in America, and the end result is equally predictable. This is the kind of thing that happens to cultural anthropologists in the field. They call it "culture shock" and cope with it by means of various rituals of detachment (this is the latent psychological function of field procedures), by staying in the company of or at least in communication with fellow outsiders to the culture being studied, and best of all by going home from the field after a relatively brief period of time. The penalty for failure in these efforts to remain outside the situation is "to go native." To be sure, cultural anthropologists like to do this behaviorally ("participant observation") and even emotionally ("empathy"). If they "go native" *cognitively*, however, they will no longer be able to do cultural anthropology. They will have dropped out of the universe of discourse in which such an enterprise is meaningful or even real.

So far, then, we have amplified the proposition concerning the demise of the supernatural in the modern world in two ways: We have conceded the empirical viability of the proposition and we have suggested that such supernaturalists as may still be around will find their beliefs buffeted by very strong social *and* psychological pressures. Therefore it is hardly surprising that a profound theological crisis exists today. The theologian like every other human being exists in a social milieu. He too is the product of socialization processes. His "knowledge" has been socially acquired, is in need of social support, and is thus vulnerable to social pressures. If the term "supernatural" is understood in the above-mentioned sense, it must be further observed that, at least traditionally, its meaningfulness has been a necessary condition of the theological enterprise. It follows that, in a situation where one may speak of a demise of the supernatural, and *where the theologian himself does so* when he describes the situation, the theological enterprise is confronted with truly formidable difficulties. The theologian more and more resembles a witch doctor stranded among logical positivists—or, of course, a logical positivist stranded among witch doctors. Willy-nilly he is exposed to the exorcisms of his cognitive antagonists. Sooner or later these exorcisms will have their effect in undermining the old certainties in his own mind.

Historical crises are rarely consummated in one dramatic moment. They are contained in processes that extend over varying periods of time and that are experienced in different ways by those affected. As Nietzsche tells us in the famous passage about the "death of God": "This tremendous event is still on its way . . . it has not yet reached the ears of man. Lightning and thunder require time, the light of the stars requires time, deeds require time even after they are done, before they can be seen and heard."[9] It would therefore be extraordinarily naïve to expect the demise of the supernatural to be equally visible from all vantage points of our culture or to be experienced in the same way by all who have taken cognizance of it. There continue to be religious and theological milieux in which the crisis is, at the most, dimly sensed as an external threat in the distance. In other milieux the crisis is beginning to be felt, but is "still on its way." In yet other milieux the crisis is in full eruption as a threat deep inside the fabric of religious practice, faith, and thought. And in some places it is as if the believer or theologian were standing in a landscape of smoldering ruins.

These differences in the perception and absorption of the crisis run across the traditional divisions between the religious groupings of Western culture. But the divisions are still significant in terms of the over-all impact of the crisis. Protestantism has lived with the crisis longest and most intensively, lived with it, that is, as an internal rather than an external cataclysm. This is because Protestant thought has always been particularly open to the spirit of modernity. Very probably this openness has its historical roots not only in an intellectual or spiritual affinity but in the important part that Protestantism actually played in the genesis of the modern world, as Max Weber and others have shown. Be this as it may, one can perceive a major trend of accommodation to modern this-worldliness in Protestant thought for well over a century, beginning as far back as 1799, when Schleiermacher's *Addresses on Religion to Its Cultured Despisers* were first published. The century that followed, extending into the present century up to World War I, saw the rise to dominance of a theological liberalism whose crucial concern was a cognitive adjustment of Christianity to the (actual or alleged) world view of modernity and one of whose major results was the progressive dismantling of the supernaturalist scaffolding of the Christian tradition. Indeed, the intended audience of Schleiermacher's *Addresses* was prophetic too. Increasingly, Protestant theology has oriented itself by changing coteries of "cultured despisers" of religion, that is, by shifting groups of secularized intellectuals whose respect it solicited and whose cognitive presuppositions it accepted as binding. In other words, Protestant theologians have been increasingly engaged in playing a game whose rules have been dictated by their cognitive antagonists. While this curious vulnerability (not to say lack of character) can probably be explained sociologically, what is interesting here is the over-all result—a profound erosion of the traditional religious contents, in extreme cases to the point where nothing is left but hollow rhetoric. Of late it seems more and more as if the extreme has become the norm.

For a short time, roughly from the end of World War I until shortly after World War II (there are some differences in the duration of this period between Europe and America, and to some extent between denominations), the trend appeared to be about to be reversed. This was the period marked by the ascent of what was variously called neo-Protestantism, dialectical theology, or (most aptly) neo-orthodoxy, ushered in with éclat in 1919 with the publication of Karl Barth's *Epistle to the Romans*. With tremendous passion Barth, particularly in his early work in the 1920s, repudiated all the major assumptions of Protestant liberalism. He called for a return to the classical faith of the Reformation, a faith that, he maintained, was unconditionally based on God's revelation and not on any human reason or experience. In retrospect it is clear that this period was an interruption rather than a reversal of the secularizing trend. It also seems likely that the interlude had a very specific historical and social-psychological foundation, namely the tremendous shocks administered to the self-confidence of the culture in general and its Christian sector in particular by the horrors of war, revolution, and economic disaster. This was, of course, especially true of German-speaking Protestantism and its confrontation with the anti-Christian delirium of Nazism. Theological liberals have gibed that neo-orthodoxy was basically a kind of postwar neurosis, a case of spiritual battle fatigue. This view has a good deal of historical plausibility. It should not surprise us, then, that the "normalization" of society setting in after World War II (in Germany this can be dated quite precisely, and in the context embarrassingly, by the currency reform of 1948) led to a rapid decline of neo-orthodoxy and to the resurgence of various strands of neo-liberalism.

More or less intact milieux of Protestant conservatism still exist, of course. These are typically located on the fringes of urban, middle-class society. They are like besieged fortresses, and their mood tends toward a militancy that only superficially covers an underlying sense of panic. At times, in eruptions of frustrated aggression, the militancy becomes hysterical. Today, the neo-orthodox, who only a few years ago could think of themselves as representing the upsurge of a new Reformation, find themselves dwindling in both numbers and influence. Most of them are elderly veterans of battles that have become unreal to the new generation (such as the battles of German Protestantism in the 1930s), and they are often even more out of touch with what animates the younger theologians than the old-line conservatives who never modified their orthodoxies with the (possibly fatal) prefix "neo-." The theological novelties that have dominated the Protestant scene in the last two decades all seem basically to take up where the older liberalism left off. This is certainly, and in these cases biographically, the case with Paul Tillich and Rudolf Bultmann. Tillich understood the task of theology as one of "correlation," by which he meant the intellectual adjustment of the Christian tradition with philosophical truth. Bultmann proposed a program of what he called "demythologization," a restatement of the biblical message in language free from the supernaturalist notions of ancient man. Both Tillich and Bultmann drew heavily on existentialism (particularly as developed in Germany by Martin Heidegger) for the concepts employed in their efforts to translate Christianity into terms adequate for modern man. The various recent movements of "radical" or "secular" theology have returned even more unambiguously to the old liberalism whether the "cultured despisers" being cognitively embraced are psychoanalysts, sociologists, existentialists, or language analysts.[10] The self-liquidation of the theological enterprise is undertaken with an enthusiasm that verges on the bizarre, culminating in the reduction to absurdity of the "God-is-dead theology" and "Christian atheism." It is no wonder that even those clergy, younger theologians, and, with particular poignancy, theological students who are not simply eager to be "with it" in terms of the latest ideological fashions are afflicted with profound malaise in this situation. The question "What next?" may sometimes be the expression of an intellectual attitude geared to fads and publicity; but it may also be a genuine cry *de profundis*. In the American situation the option of political activity, made morally reasonable by the unspeakable mess of our domestic and international affairs, can serve as a welcome relief, a liberating "leap" from ambiguity to commitment. I do not for one moment wish to disparage this option, but it should be clear from even moderate reflection that the fundamental *cognitive* problem will not be solved in this manner.

The Catholic situation is different, at least in part because Catholicism has viewed the modern world with much more suspicion from the beginning and, as a result, has managed to keep up its cognitive defenses against modernity more effectively and until a much more recent date. Throughout the nineteenth century, while Protestant liberalism carried on its great love affair with the spirit of the age, the basic temper of Catholicism can be described as a magnificent defiance. This temper is exemplified by the figure of Pius IX, whose *Syllabus of Errors* of 1864 condemned, among other modern abominations, the claim that "the Roman Pontiff can and ought to reconcile himself to, and agree with, progress, liberalism and civilization as lately introduced." It was in the same pontificate that the First Vatican Council proclaimed papal infallibility as well as the immaculate conception, in July 1870 in the very teeth of "civilization as lately introduced," which, two months later, marched into Rome in the shape of Victor Emmanuel's army. As late as 1950 (on the very eve of sputnik, as it were) this splendid recalcitrance in the face of modernity manifested itself once more in the proclamation of the dogma of the bodily assumption of Mary into heaven. But that was in the pontificate of Pius XII. The winds of change began to blow more wildly under John XXIII.

It goes without saying that there were undercurrents of accommodation and modernization long before this. The very constitution of the Catholic church, however, provided the means by which these currents could, indeed, be kept *under.* Thus the whole syndrome of secularization, including the demise of the supernatural, could be officially diagnosed as a malady of the world outside the gates. On the inside, the supernaturalist apparatus of mystery and miracle could go on as before—just as long as the defenses (political as well as cognitive) were properly manned, or so it seemed. Such fifth columns within the church as, for instance, the modernist movement around the turn of the century were promptly and effectively repressed. In this particular instance the Freudian allegory of hydraulics is most apt: The repressed impulses, when finally released, threaten to blow off the roof. The pumps, of course, began to gush with Vatican II. The ancient dikes showed punctures. Not that there were no little boys ready and willing to stick their fingers into all the holes —the conservatives were, and did. And now, when all the furniture seems to be swimming out to sea, they can say with some justice, "We told you so."

The theological flux that has engulfed large segments of Catholicism since Vatican II is still very new. There are still sizable islands of immunity, especially in geographical or social areas that are relatively sheltered from modern mass communications (not to speak of literacy). But in Catholic intellectual milieux, the very milieux in which the theological enterprise must be socially rooted, there have of late emerged noises of a fearful modernity sufficient to put the most "radical" Protestant to shame. David Martin, a British sociologist of religion, has described this process with admirable succinctness: "Most Protestant countries in the Anglo-Saxon ambit have been so used to religious vacuity that another cloud of existentialist dust barely disturbs the clarity of their theological vision. But for those only lately inured to clear and distinct ideas like Thomism or to the firm exercise of authority, the effect is startling. Just as Catholics who cease to be conservative often become Marxists so those who cease to be Thomist easily embrace the most extreme existentialist fashion. They are experts at excluding the middle."[11] In other words, in religion as in politics, if one once starts to clobber the opposition, one stops clobbering at one's peril. The peril was predictable. The irony of the situation is that the Catholic liberals, who rank sociology high in their hierarchy of secular revelations, have failed to see the peril. The conservatives, who generally view sociology as one of the more nefarious devilries of modern intellect, smelled the danger signals a mile off. It may well be that conservatives usually have the better sociological noses.

The Jews have experienced the crisis differently. For one thing, Judaism, unlike Christianity, has never developed authoritative and rigorously defined systems of theological propositions. Orthodoxy in Judaism has always been more a matter of practice than of belief. An orthodox Jew can hold any number of perhaps wildly modernistic ideas without necessarily feeling that these are inconsistent with his attitudes regarding family excursions on Saturday or family meals with certain kinds of salami. Thus the efforts of Mordecai Kaplan to "reconstruct" Judaism by getting rid of its entire baggage of traditional supernaturalism, while enraging a goodly number of his fellow rabbis, created less of a storm among American Jews than a comparable program would have, certainly at the time of its initial promulgation in the 1930s, in most Christian milieux. For another thing, Judaism, unlike any Western form of Christianity, has an ethnic dimension, which is closely related to its religious tradition but may also be divorced from it. The modern crisis of Judaism has been closely linked to the so-called problem of Jewish identity, and there have been various strictly secular solutions to this, the most successful having been political Zionism. Nevertheless secularization has plunged Judaism into a dilemma as great as Christianity's. It is all very well to say that Judaism is, above all, a matter of practice. This practice is, however, rooted in a specific cognitive universe without which it is threatened with meaninglessness. The numerous pre- and proscriptions of orthodox Judaism are likely to appear as so many absurdities, unless they remain linked to a world view that includes the supernatural. Lacking this, despite all sorts of traditional loyalties and nostalgias, the whole edifice of traditional piety takes on the character of a museum of religious history. People may like museums, but they are reluctant to live in them. And the secular solutions to the problem of Jewish identity become highly tenuous unless there is *either* anti-Semitic pressure *or* a "natural" Jewish community to which the individual can belong regardless of his religious orientation. The decline of both conditions in contemporary America has produced considerable worries for American Jewish leadership. In Israel, where the second condition pertains, the debates, extending into legal controversy, over the relationship of Jewishness, Judaism, and Israeli nationality indicate the appearance of new variations of the classical problem of identity. In neither country does it seem plausible to exempt Judaism as a religion from the crisis that interests us here.[12]

As we have seen, the crisis is refracted in different ways through the several prisms of religious traditions, but no tradition within the orbit of modern Western societies is exempt from it. A good case can also be made (though not here) that religious traditions in non-Western societies that are undergoing modernization become engulfed in the same crisis, the extent of the crisis keeping pace with the extent of modernization.

In this confrontation between religion and modernity the case of Protestantism is the prototype. Both Catholic and Jewish writers in America have referred to the "Protestantization" of their respective communities, by which they usually mean certain features of their community life (for example, the development of the church as a social center for its congregation, or the emergence of the clergy into public life on certain current issues) that can be attributed to Protestant influence. The term, however, has deeper implications. The case of Protestantism may well serve other religious traditions as a highly instructive example of the impact of the crisis and its various effects. It was Protestantism that first underwent the onslaught of secularization; Protestantism that first adapted itself to societies in which several faiths existed on equal terms, the pluralism may be regarded as a twin phenomenon to secularization,[13] and it was in Protestant theology that the cognitive challenges to traditional supernaturalism were first met and fought through. The Protestant experience has a vicarious quality about it, especially in its assorted miseries. Catholic and Jewish writers, who on occasion are prone to be patronizing about these miseries, might do well to watch the portents and to realize that they are in no way immune to the same perils.

How one predicts the future course of the secularizing trend obviously depends to a large extent on how one explains the origins and the moving forces of the trend to begin with. There are many different theories of the roots of secularization,[14] but whether one sees the process in terms of the history of ideas (listing factors such as the growth of scientific rationalism or the latent secularity of biblical religion itself), or whether one prefers more sociologically oriented theories (with factors such as industrialization, urbanization, or the pluralism of social milieux), it is difficult to see why any of these elements should suddenly reverse themselves. It is more reasonable to assume that a high degree of secularization is a cultural concomitant of modern industrial societies, at least as we now know them, so that abrupt changes in the secularizing trend are not very likely in the foreseeable future. This presupposes what Kahn and Wiener rather nicely call a "surprise-free" world, that is, a world in which present trends continue to unfold without the intrusion of totally new and unexpected factors.

Our "futurologists" themselves seem a little nervous about the notion of "surprise-freeness," and with good reason. One might wonder whether someone equipped with the techniques of modern social science in the late fifteenth century would have been in a position to predict the imminence of the Reformation—or a similarly precocious type in the late first century the coming expansion of Christianity. One of the elements that keeps history from being a complete bore is that it is full of "surprises." At the present time it is easy to envision a number of possible "surprises" that would mean that all bets are off, with regard to secularization or any other present trend—a thermonuclear war devastating much of the world, a complete collapse of the capitalist economic system, permanent racial war in America, and so on. If any of these are in store for us, attempts at prognosis are futile. It would hardly help our understanding to predict the appearance of strange new religions among the wretched survivors of a thermonuclear Armageddon. We lack the data to play through, in the case of religion, what Kahn and Wiener call "canonical variations," that is, possible constellations of "surprise" developments. But despite these limitations, some further observations are possible. We can assume the continuation of the secularizing trend and then proceed to ask what options this leaves for religion and theological thought—options that will, of course, have to be exercised under the conditions of a cognitive minority.

The fundamental option is simple: It is a choice between hanging on to or surrendering cognitive deviance. This choice belongs to the realm of ideas. But it is very important to understand that it has practical social implications.

Choices in real life are rarely pure, but to understand the middle ground it is helpful to imagine the extremes. At one extreme, then, is the option to maintain (or possibly to reconstruct) a supernaturalist position in the teeth of a cognitively antagonistic world. This entails an attitude of the stiff upper lip, a steadfast refusal to "go native," a (literally or otherwise) pontifical insouciance about the opinions of mankind. The theologian with this stance will stick to his trade, supernaturalism and all, and the world (literally or otherwise) be damned. Assuming the continuation of the secularizing trend, this stance is not going to get any easier to maintain. There will be extremely strong social and social-psychological pressures against it. Unless our theologian has the inner fortitude of a desert saint, he has only one effective remedy against the threat of cognitive collapse in the face of these pressures: He must huddle together with like-minded fellow deviants —and huddle very closely indeed. Only in a countercommunity of considerable strength does cognitive deviance have a chance to maintain itself. The countercommunity provides continuing therapy against the creeping doubt as to whether, after all, one may not be wrong and the majority right. To ʿulfill its function of providing social support for the deviant body of "knowledge," the countercommunity must provide a strong sense of solidarity among its members (a "fellowship of the saints" in a world rampant with devils) and it must be quite closed vis-à-vis the outside ("Be not yoked together with unbelievers!"). In sum, it must be a kind of ghetto.

People may be forced into ghettos, or they may elect to live in them. It is relevant to recall that Judaism originally created the ghetto as a segregated countercommunity, not because of outside coercion, but because of its own religious necessities. Probably as far back as the Babylonian exile the segregated Jewish community was the social expression (and, one may add, a sociologically necessary one) of the separateness, the difference of the Jewish religion. Without the fence of the law, as the rabbis well realized, Judaism could not have survived in the midst of the Gentiles. Inevitably this theological fence had to produce a practical social analogue. But to live in a fenced-in milieu requires strong motivation. In the absence of such motivation, only persecution or outside force can produce the social conditions necessary for the survival of the cognitive deviance.

When people themselves elect to live in this kind of segregation from the larger society we have the phenomenon that sociologists have analyzed as sectarianism. The term "sect" is used in different ways in common speech. Sociologically, it means a religious group that is relatively small, in tension with the larger society and closed (one might say "balled up") against it, and that makes very strong claims on the loyalty and solidarity of its members. The choice to persist in defiant cognitive deviance necessarily also entails the choice of sectarian forms of social organization. But people must somehow be motivated to live in such sects. Sometimes this can happen "naturally," if the sectarian or ghetto community coincides with ethnic or class barriers set up by the larger society. This happened for a while with Catholicism in the United States, but as the barriers began to come down the sectarian motives declined in the same measure. Sometimes the larger society may be so unattractive that the sectarian underworld has an appeal over and beyond its particular message. This probably helps to account for the period of neo-orthodox ascendancy in European Protestantism. In a world full of Nazis one can be forgiven for being a Barthian.

The trouble with the sectarian option, at least in a

"surprise-free" projection of the future, is that such "favorable" circumstances are not very likely to recur. Social mobility and integration are likely to increase, not recede. Modern governments are unlikely to start imposing religious conformity after a long-lasting trend in the opposite direction. Even the most fundamentalist Marxists seem to be losing their taste for religious persecution. The resulting conditions are not only unfavorable to the maintenance of religious monopolies in any sizable segments of the society, they also produce an open market for world views, religious or secular, in which sects have a hard time thriving.[15] In other words, the modern situation is conducive to open systems of "knowledge" in competition and communication with each other, and not to the closed structures in which widely deviant "knowledge" can be cultivated.

The option of cognitive defiance, then, runs into considerable difficulties of "social engineering." To these must be added, in the case of the major Christian groups, a profound aversion to sectarian forms. Christianity has behind it many centuries of universalism and social establishment. The suggestion to go underground, as it were, is unlikely to recommend itself to many churchmen or theologians, least of all in the Catholic camp. The odd sound and indeed literally contradictory meaning of the phrases "Catholic sect" or "sectarian Catholicism" reveal the fundamental spiritual incompatibility.

The polar opposite of defiance is surrender. In this option the cognitive authority and superiority of whatever is taken to be "the *Weltanschauung* of modern man" is conceded with few if any reservations. Modernity is swallowed hook, line, and sinker, and the repast is accompanied by a sense of awe worthy of Holy Communion. Indeed, the sense of injury and incomprehension evinced by modernist theologians whose cognitive celebration is rejected could well be put in the words of the Anglican *Book of Common Prayer*, in the pre-Communion exhortation to negligent parishioners: "Ye know how grievous and unkind a thing it is, when a man hath prepared a rich feast, decked his table with all kind of provision, so that there lacketh nothing but the guests to sit down: and yet they who are called . . . most unthankfully refuse to come." At the moment, of course, there is little reason to complain on this score—the feast lacketh not in attendance.

The basic intellectual task undertaken as a result of this option is one of *translation*. The traditional religious affirmations are translated into terms appropriate to the new frame of reference, the one that allegedly conforms to the *Weltanschauung* of modernity. Different translation grammars have been employed for this purpose, depending on the preferences of the theologians in question as well as their different notions as to the character of the modern *Weltanschauung*. In the cases of Paul Tillich and Rudolf Bultmann, the grammars are variants of existentialism. In the more recent American derivations of "radical" theology, some sort of Jungian psychology, linguistic philosophy, and popular sociology have been used to accomplish the translation. Whatever the differences in method, the result is very similar in all these cases: The supernatural elements of the religious traditions are more or less completely liquidated, and the traditional language is transferred from other-worldly to this-worldly referents. The traditional lore, and in most cases the religious institution in charge of this lore as well, can then be presented as still or again "relevant" to modern man.

It goes without saying that these procedures require a good deal of intellectual contortionism. The major sociological difficulty, however, lies elsewhere. The various forms of secularized theology, unless they are understood as individual intellectual exercises (something against which the ecclesiastical background of most of their protagonists militates), propose various practical pay-offs. Typically, the lay recipient of these blessings will be either a happier person (his existential anxieties assuaged or his archetypal needs fulfilled) or a more effective citizen (usually this means a bigger and better political liberal), or perhaps both. The trouble is that these benefits are also available under strictly secular labels. A secularized Christianity (and, for that matter, a secularized Judaism) has to go to considerable exertion to demonstrate that the religious label, as modified in conformity with the spirit of the age, has anything special to offer. Why should one buy psychotherapy or racial liberalism in a "Christian" package, when the same commodities are available under purely secular and for that very reason even more modernistic labels? The preference for the former will probably be limited to people with a sentimental nostalgia for traditional symbols—a group that, under the influence of the secularizing theologians, is steadily dwindling. For most people, symbols whose content has been hollowed out lack conviction or even interest. In other words, the theological surrender to the alleged demise of the supernatural defeats itself in precisely the measure of its success. Ultimately, it represents the self-liquidation of theology and of the institutions in which the theological tradition is embodied.

Extreme choices are, however, not only relatively rare, they are particularly unlikely to be adopted by sizable institutions with a variety of vested interests in social survival. There may be coteries of intellectuals to whom something like "Christian atheism" has an appeal, but a banner with this strange device is unlikely to be taken up by any of the major churches. Conversely, the extreme of defiant traditionalism is likely to be restricted to smaller groups, typically those whose social location (in "backward" regions, say, or in the lower classes) gives them little interest or stake in the world of modernity. The larger religious groups are rather inclined toward various forms and degrees of *aggiornamento*, that is of limited, controlled accommodation. Cognitively, this stance involves a bargaining process with modern thought, a surrender of some traditional (which here equals supernatural) items while others are kept.

This was the classical pattern of Protestant theological liberalism. Under new guises it has come to the fore again, in Protestantism since World War II and in Catholicism since Vatican II. While this pattern has the healthiest prospects in terms of social survival values, it has its own troubles too. The main one is a built-in escalation factor—escalation, that is, toward the pole of cognitive surrender. *Aggiornamento* usually arises out of tactical considerations. It is argued that one must modify certain features of the institution or its message because otherwise one will not be able to reach this or that recalcitrant clientele—the intelligentsia, or the working class, or the young. These modifications, however, entail a process of *rethinking*, the end results of which are hard to predict or control. Tactical modifications thus tend to escalate toward genuinely cognitive modifications. At this point the outside challenge becomes a challenge from within. The cognitive antagonist has crept inside the gates and, worse, inside the consciousness of the theologian assigned to guard the gates. The notion that trade promotes understanding is a sound one. When one trades ideas, however, the understanding pushes toward agreement, for those reasons deeply grounded in man's social nature that have been mentioned before. In other words, once one starts a process of cognitive bargaining, one subjects oneself to mutual cognitive contamination. The crucial question then is, Who is the stronger party? If the secularization thesis holds, the stronger party, of course, is the modern world in which the supernatural has become irrelevant. The theologian who trades ideas with the modern world, therefore, is likely to come out with a poor bargain, that is, he will probably have to give far more than he will get. To vary the image, he who sups with the devil had better have a long spoon. The devilry of modernity has its own magic: The theologian who sups with *it* will find his spoon getting shorter and shorter—until that last supper in which he is left alone at the table, with no spoon at all and with an empty plate. The devil, one may guess, will by then have gone away to more interesting company.

Having considered the options and their likely consequences on the "surprise-free" prognosis that the secularizing trend will continue as before, it may be useful now to look briefly at some possible modifications of the trend short of the cataclysmic possibilities in which any prognosis would come to nought. Dean Inge once remarked that a man who marries the spirit of the age soon finds himself a widower. This can be the result of external events, and sometimes happens quite suddenly. For example, as recently as 1965 Harvey Cox in *The Secular City* invited us to celebrate the advent of modern urbanism as if it were some sort of divine revelation. Only a few years later it is difficult to rouse much enthusiasm for *this* particular bit of "timely" wisdom. American cities seem fated to go up in flame in an annual ritual of mad destructiveness and futility. The civil rights movement, which presumably gave Cox confidence in the libertarian future of urban secularity, seems dead as a political force. And that larger city, which is the American polity, has been bled of its moral substance in the war in Vietnam. Right now very few people in America are in a mood to celebrate much of anything in their city. The lesson of this example can be augmented by a look into even the nearest future. It is quite possible that the Vietnamese war will end in the near future, even end abruptly, and that its termination will be followed by policies that come closer to sanity and humaneness. It is also possible that the war will go on for a long time or, even worse, that one Vietnam will follow another in a series of imperial adventures. If "timeliness" is the criterion, how are Christians to follow Cox's admonition to "speak politically"? In the stirring notes of millenarian optimism that marked the early civil rights movement? Or in the apocalyptic mood that seems more appropriate right now? Depending upon how things go, the one or the other option could become obsolete in no time at all. "Relevance" is a very fragile business at best.

It is not only the vagaries and sudden turns of external events that make it so. The organization of our cultural life creates a fragility. Relevance and timeliness are defined for the society at large, primarily by the media of mass communication. These are afflicted with an incurable hunger for novelty. The relevancies they proclaim are, almost by definition, extremely vulnerable to changing fashions and thus of generally short duration. As a result, the theologian (or, of course, any other intellectual) who seeks to be and remain "with it," in terms of mass-communicated and mass-communicable relevance, is predestined to find himself authoritatively put down as irrelevant very soon. Those who consider themselves too sophisticated for mass culture take their cues on relevance and timeliness from an assortment of intellectual cliques, which have their own communications system, characterized by fashions that are more intolerant but hardly more durable than those of the mass media. In this country the maharajas of the world of true sophistication are mainly individuals whose baptism in secularity has been by total immersion. The theologian who wants to take his cues from this source is unlikely even to be recognized short of abject capitulation to the realities taken for granted in these particular circles—realities hardly conducive to the theological enterprise in any form. But even he who is ready for such capitulation should be cautioned. Intellectuals are notoriously haunted by boredom (they like to call this "alienation" nowadays). Our intellectual maharajas are no exception, if only because they mainly talk to each other. There is no telling what outlandish religiosity, even one dripping with savage supernaturalism, may yet arise in these groups, which will once more leave our theologian where he started, on the outside of the cocktail party, looking in.

But let us assume that theological relevance is oriented by long-term social trends rather than by fleeting fashions, eso- or exoteric. Even here a little caution is in order. There is scattered evidence that secularization may not be as all-embracing as some have thought, that the supernatural, banished from cognitive respectability by the intellectual authorities, may survive in hidden nooks and crannies of the culture. Some, for that matter, are not all that hidden. There continue to be quite massive manifestations of that sense of the uncanny that modern rationalism calls "superstition"—last but not least in the continuing and apparently flourishing existence of an astrological subculture! For whatever reasons, sizable numbers of the specimen "modern man" have not lost a propensity for awe, for the uncanny, for all those possibilities that are legislated against by the canons of secularized rationality.[16] These subterranean rumblings of supernaturalism can, it seems, coexist with all sorts of upstairs rationalism. In a study of American students, 80 per cent of the respondents expressed a "need for religious faith," while only 48 per cent admitted to a belief in God in traditional Judaeo-Christian terms.[17] Even more startling, in a recent opinion poll conducted in western Germany, 68 per cent said that they believed in God—but 86 per cent admitted to praying![18] There are different ways of interpreting such data. They can perhaps be explained quite simply in terms of mankind's chronic illogicality. But perhaps they express a more significant discrepancy between verbal assent to the truisms of modernity and an actual world view of much greater complexity. In this connection the following data give one pause:

According to studies made in England, nearly 50 per cent of the respondents had consulted a fortuneteller, one in six believed in ghosts—and one in fifteen claimed to have seen one![19]

I would shy away from any explanations, such as those made in a Jungian vein, in terms of the psychology of religion, that is, in terms of alleged religious "needs" that are frustrated by modern culture and seek an outlet in some way. Empirically, the psychological premises here are very dubious. Theologically, there are few ideas less helpful than the one that religious belief relates to religious need as orgasm does to lust. And it is not unthinkable, after all, that in a world as poorly arranged as this one we may be afflicted with "needs" that are doomed to frustration except in illusion (which, of course, is what Freud thought). However, psychology apart, it is possible to argue that the human condition, fraught as it is with suffering and with the finality of death, demands interpretations that not only satisfy theoretically but give inner sustenance in meeting the crisis of suffering and death. In Max Weber's sense of the term, there is a need, social rather than psychological, for *theodicy*. Theodicy (literally, "justification of God") originally referred to theories that sought to explain how an all-powerful and all-good God can permit suffering and evil in the world. Weber used the term more broadly for any theoretical explanation of the meaning of suffering or evil.

There are, of course, secular theodicies. They fail, however, in interpreting and thus in making bearable the extremes of human suffering. They fail notably in interpreting death. The Marxist case is instructive. The Marxist theory of history does, indeed, provide a kind of theodicy: All things will be made whole in the postrevolutionary utopia. This can be quite comforting to an individual facing death on the barricades. Such a death is meaningful in terms of the theory. But the wisdom of Marxism is unlikely to afford much comfort to an individual facing a cancer operation. The death he faces is strictly meaningless within this (and, indeed, any) frame of reference of theodicy slanted toward this world. These remarks are not, at this point, intended as an argument for the truth of religion. Perhaps the truth is comfortless and without ultimate meaning for human hope. Sociologically speaking, however, the stoicism that can embrace this kind of truth is rare. Most people, it seems, want a greater comfort, and so far it has been religious theodicies that have provided it.

There are therefore some grounds for thinking that, at the very least, pockets of supernaturalist religion are likely to survive in the larger society. As far as the religious communities are concerned, we may expect a revulsion against the more grotesque extremes of self-liquidation of the supernaturalist traditions. It is a fairly reasonable prognosis that in a "surprise-free" world the global trend of secularization will continue. An impressive rediscovery of the supernatural, in the dimensions of a mass phenomenon, is not in the books. At the same time, significant enclaves of supernaturalism within the secularized culture will also continue. Some of these may be remnants of traditionalism, of the sort that sociologists like to analyze in terms of cultural lag. Others may be new groupings, possible locales for a rediscovery of the supernatural. Both types will have to organize themselves in more or less sectarian social forms. The large religious bodies are likely to continue their tenuous quest for a middle ground between traditionalism and *aggiornamento*, with both sectarianism and secularizing dissolution nibbling away at the edges. This is not a dramatic picture, but it is more likely than the prophetic visions of either the end of religion or a coming age of resurrected gods.

If my aim here were primarily sociological analysis or prognosis, this would be the end of the argument. Since this is not the case in this book, the preceding is in the nature of preliminary discussion. It is intended to delineate some facets of the situation within which thinking about religion must take place today. I am concerned with the religious questions themselves, on the level of truth rather than timeliness. I also contend (as I will explain next) that the sociological perspective on these questions can yield a little more than a diagnosis of the present situation. No one, to be sure, can think about religion or anything else in sovereign independence of his situation in time and space. The history of human thought demonstrates rather clearly, however, that it is possible to go some way in asking questions of truth while disregarding the spirit of an age, and even to arrive at answers that contradict this spirit. Genuine timeliness means sensitivity to one's socio-historical starting point, *not* fatalism about one's possible destination. What follows, then, is based on the belief that it is possible to liberate oneself to a considerable degree from the taken-for-granted assumptions of one's time. This belief has as its correlate an ultimate indifference to the majority or minority status of one's view of the world, an indifference that is equally removed from the exaltation of being fully "with it" and from the arrogance of esotericism. Perhaps this indifference also has an element of contempt for the emotional satisfactions of either stance.

2. The Perspective of Sociology: Relativizing the Relativizers

Knowledge can be cultivated for its own sake; it can also have very definite existential consequences. It is possible to make the case that existentially (that is, in terms of the individual's existence in the world) true knowledge leads to experiences of ecstasy—of *ek-stasis*, a standing outside of the taken-for-granted routines of everyday life. Bodies and modes of knowledge differ, both in the degree to which they are conducive to such ecstasy and in the character of the ecstasy they provide. There are kinds of knowledge that appear to be quite timeless in this respect; for example, the knowledge of the tragic poet. We can turn from the daily newspaper to Aeschylus or Shakespeare and discover that the insights of the tragedians actually pertain to the events of the day—and the ecstasy thus achieved can, indeed, be a terrifying one.

There are other kinds of knowledge that provide ecstasies of a more timely character. For example, the discovery of the complexity of each individual's subjectivity that gave birth to the novel as a literary form in the modern West is timely and time-bound in a quite different way. We can be moved to ecstasy by Shakespeare, and the Elizabethans could be so moved by Aeschylus, but it is very doubtful that the ecstatic insights of Balzac or Dostoyevsky could have been grasped in the sixteenth century. Conversely, modern Western man appears to have practically lost the capacity to comprehend, let alone to replicate, the ecstatic condition that the practices of various religious cults provided for their members throughout most of previous human history.

Theological thought, which is in the ecstasy business almost by definition, is inevitably affected by the kinds of knowledge that bring about the peculiar ecstasies of the time —regardless of whether these ecstasies are true or false ones by some extraneous criteria of validity, and pretty much regardless of whether theological thought seeks out or resists the same ecstasies. The sociological reasons for this have already been discussed. Another reason is the intrinsic human propensity for unified thought. Honest, sustained reflection recoils from cognitive schizophrenia. It seeks to unify, to reconcile, to understand how one thing taken as truth relates to another so taken. In the history of Christian thought each age has presented its own peculiar challenges to the theologian. Our own age differs only in the acceleration in the sequence of challenges. Not surprisingly, the theologian in our situation is haunted by a sense of vertigo, though he is hardly alone in this affliction.

Marx, in a pun on the German meaning of the name Feuerbach, once said that anyone doing serious philosophy in that time would first have to pass through the "fiery brook" of Feuerbach's thought. Today the sociological perspective constitutes the "fiery brook" through which the theologian must pass—or, perhaps more accurately, ought to pass. It is sociological thought, and most acutely the sociology of knowledge, that offers the specifically contemporary challenge to theology. Theology can, of course, ignore this challenge. It is always possible to avoid challenges, sometimes for a long time. It might be argued, for example, that Hindu thought has managed to avoid the challenge of Buddhism for some twenty-five hundred years. All the same, there are challenges that one avoids at a peril—not necessarily a practical one, but a peril to the integrity of one's thought. In this particular case, because of the crisis discussed previously, avoiding the challenge of sociology will almost certainly have nefarious practical as well as cognitive consequences.

In a broad sense of the term, this is the latest embodiment of the challenge of modern scientific thought. Seen in this context, sociology is simply the most recent in a series of scientific disciplines that have profoundly challenged theology. The physical sciences were probably first in the line of attack, and it is they that first occur to most people when a scientific challenge to theology is mentioned. People think of

Copernicus and Galileo, of the challenge to the cosmology of the Middle Ages, particularly to the central position in the universe it assigned to men and man's earth, and, more recently, of the rationally explicable universe of modern physics, in which the "religious hypothesis" becomes increasingly unnecessary to explain reality. However valid the actual conflict between theology and the physical sciences may or may not be, there is no doubt that such a conflict has been profoundly believed to exist, and the over-all effect of this belief has been related to what Max Weber aptly called the disenchantment of the world.

The revolution in biology during the nineteenth century further aggravated the challenge. If Copernicus dethroned man cosmologically, Darwin dethroned him even more painfully biologically. It has been fashionable to relish these metaphysical humiliations of man and to look with superior amusement at the efforts of the backward souls who tried to resist accepting them. Backward they may have been, but hardly amusing. The joke, if anything, is on us. In that case, it is a grim joke. There is really nothing very funny about finding oneself stranded, alone, in a remote corner of a universe bereft of human meaning—nor about the idea that this fate is the outcome of the mindless massacre that Darwin, rather euphemistically, called natural selection. My own sympathies, I must confess, are with the pathetic rear-guard action of William Jennings Bryan rather than with the insipid progress-happiness of Clarence Darrow—an admirable man in many ways, but one dense enough sincerely to believe that a Darwinist view of man could serve as a basis for his opposition to capital punishment.

Contrary to the popular assumptions, I would, however, argue that the physical sciences' challenges to the theology have been *relatively* mild. They have challenged certain literal interpretations of the Bible, such as the belief that the universe was created in seven literal days or that the human race is literally descended from Adam. But such beliefs can, after all, be plausibly interpreted as not touching upon the essence of faith. More serious is that general disenchantment of the world mentioned before, but the very sense of abandonment this brings about can also become a motive for passionate theological affirmations—as the examples of Pascal and Kierkegaard demonstrate. The challenges of the human sciences, on the other hand, have been more critical, more dangerous to the essence of the theological enterprise. Sociology's two important predecessors were, successively, history and psychology. It was historical scholarship, especially as it developed in the nineteenth century, that first threatened to undermine theology at its very roots. Its challenge, too, began with details that could more or less plausibly be dismissed as trivial—the discovery of different sources for biblical books that had been canonized as unities, or of inconsistencies in the several accounts of the life of Jesus. All these details, however, came to add up to something much more serious— a pervasive sense of the historical character of *all* elements of the tradition, which significantly weakened the latter's claims to uniqueness and authority. Put simply, historical scholarship led to a perspective in which even the most sacrosanct elements of religious tradition came to be seen as *human products*. Psychology deepened this challenge, because it suggested that the production could be not only seen but explained. Rightly or wrongly, psychology after Freud suggested that religion was a gigantic projection of human needs and desires—a suggestion all the more sinister because of the unedifying character of these needs and desires, and finally sinister because of the allegedly unconscious mechanisms of the projection process. Thus history and psychology together plunged theology into a veritable vortex of relativizations. The resulting crisis in credibility has engulfed the theological enterprise *in toto*, not merely this or that detail of interpretation.

This is not the place for a critique of the final validity of these challenges. I, for one, take the claims of history more seriously than those of psychology. Be this as it may, the challenge of sociology can be seen as a further intensification of the crisis. The historical nature and product-character, and thus the relativity rather than absolutism, of the religious traditions becomes even more transparent as the social dynamics of their historical production is understood. And the notion of projection becomes much more plausible in its sociological rather than its psychological form, because the former is simpler and more readily verifiable in ordinary, "conscious" experience. Sociology, it may be said, raises the vertigo of relativity to its most furious pitch, posing a challenge to theological thought with unprecedented sharpness.

What are the dimensions of this challenge?

The more obvious dimension is that sociological research gives the theologian a sense of his own minority status in contemporary society. One can, of course, maintain that, here as elsewhere, sociology simply belabors what everyone knows already. After all, the decline of religion in the modern world had been noted, hailed, and bewailed before any sociologists started to investigate the matter. Nevertheless there is a difference between very general, unsubstantiated observations about the alleged spirit of the age and the kind of sober specific data that sociology habitually digs up. For example, it had certainly been known for a long time that the big city is not conducive to traditional piety. But careful statistical data on this subject, such as those accumulated by Gabriel LeBras in his studies of Catholic practice in France, have quite a different shock effect. This was expressed dramatically in LeBras' well-known statement that a certain railroad station in Paris appears to have a magical quality, for rural migrants seem to be changed from practicing to nonpracticing Catholics the very moment they set foot in it.

It is very hard to estimate the over-all effect of sociological information as it is diffused in a certain milieu—in this case to judge how important such information has been in the radical rethinking of its own position that has been going on in French Catholicism since World War II. It is obvious, however, that such data as those of LeBras and his school give an altogether different dimension, namely one of scientific verifiability, to such statements as the one that France is in fact mission territory—a statement that was, among other things, influential in starting the worker-priest movement.[20] To take another example, it has probably been common knowledge for a long time that American Protestant ministers were careful of the views of their congregations and that this cautiousness increased with the degree of their professional success. But it is still rather shocking when this fact is brought out with careful documentation, as was done in a study of ministers in the racial crisis in Little Rock.[21]

The shock effect is often unintended. It can begin with very modest, practical questions. A minister, say, wants to find out how well he is getting across to his congregation in his sermons. He decides on a little do-it-yourself sociological research and hands out a questionnaire. The answers come back and show that the greater part of the congregation do not seem to have heard his preaching at all. They agree and disagree, on the questionnaire, with things he never said. This has really happened, by the way, and it is not hard to see that such information would be greatly disturbing to a minister. Let us assume that his curiosity is stirred more deeply now and he proceeds with his research activities. He might next discover that what many in his congregation mean by religion has very little relationship to what he means or to the denominational tradition to which the congregation claims allegiance. He might also find that his own role is understood by members of the congregation in a way that is diametrically opposed to his self-understanding. He thinks he is preaching the gospel, they believe he is providing moral instruction for their children. He wants to have an impact on their social and political beliefs, they want him to stay away from these and edify their family life. And so on. What began with some practical questions on how to be a more effective minister ends with information that puts in question the whole business of ministry and church. Variations of such a process of increasingly alarming insights are far from uncommon in America today and have contributed to the over-all nervousness of the clergy.

There is a certain cruel irony in this, especially in view of the fact that a good deal of the work in the sociology of religion begins as market research undertaken on behalf of religious organizations. The lesson, perhaps, is that one calls on the sociologist at one's peril. One may do so, initially, for the most pragmatic reasons, simply wanting to get information that will be useful in the planning and execution of institutional policies. One may find that, without anyone's (including the sociologist's) desiring it, the information that emerges subverts some basic presuppositions of the institution itself. One is tempted to suggest that sociologists offering their services to institutional bureaucracies pronounce a loud *caveat emptor* before they start working.

There is, however, a more profound dimension to the challenge of sociology to theological thought. This is the dimension of the sociology of knowledge.[22] Its challenge to theological thought lies in its ability to provide a kind of *answer* to the problem of relativity. The answer, though, is not exactly comforting, at least not at first blush.

The sociology of knowledge, a subdiscipline of sociology that began in Germany in the 1920s and was made familiar to English-speaking sociologists through the writings of Karl Mannheim, is concerned with studying the relationship between human thought and the social conditions under which it occurs. Its basic relevance to the subject at hand can be illustrated fairly easily by explaining the concept of plausibility structures.

One of the fundamental propositions of the sociology of knowledge is that the plausibility, in the sense of what people actually find credible, of views of reality depends upon the social support these receive. Put more simply, we obtain our notions about the world originally from other human beings, and these notions continue to be plausible to us in a very large measure because others continue to affirm them. There are some exceptions to this—notions that derive directly and instantaneously from our own sense experience— but even these can be integrated into meaningful views of reality only by virtue of social processes. It is, of course, possible to go against the social consensus that surrounds us, but there are powerful pressures (which manifest themselves as psychological pressures within our own consciousness) to conform to the views and beliefs of our fellow men. It is in conversation, in the broadest sense of the word, that we build up and keep going our view of the world. It follows that this view will depend upon the continuity and consistency of such conversation, and that it will change as we change conversation partners.

We all exist within a variety of social networks or conversational fabrics, which are related in often complex and sometimes contradictory ways with our various conceptions of the universe. When we get to the more sophisticated of these conceptions, there are likely to be organized practices designed to still doubts and prevent lapses of conviction. These practices are called therapies. There are also likely to be more or less systematized explanations, justifications, and theories in support of the conceptions in question. These sociologists have called legitimations.

For example, every society, including our own, organizes the sexual life of its members. Some sexual practices are permitted and even sanctified, others are forbidden and execrated. If all goes well (and that generally means if there are no failures in the socialization of individuals) people will do what they are supposed to do in this area and stay away from the tabu possibilities. The males will, say, marry the women they desire most and refrain from sleeping with each other. But not everything goes well all the time. Occasionally, somebody slips from the straight and narrow path. Society may punish him for this, using the various mechanisms that sociologists call social controls; it may also seek to "help" him. The therapeutic or "helping" agencies will point out his errors and offer him a way of coming back into the fold. In our society, there is a vast network of psychotherapists, counselors, and social workers with just this function. Even when things go well, however, people sometimes ask questions. They want explanations for the moral imperatives that society inflicts on them. These explanations, or legitimations, are designed to convince people that what they are being told to do is not only the prudent thing, but also the only right and salutary one. Many psychologists have performed this trick by identifying socially enjoined sexual behavior with "mental health." In a social situation containing all these therapeutic and legitimating defenses it becomes quite plausible, at least most of the time, to get married and to abhor homosexuality. It would be very different if a society defined "normality" in a different way and imposed this other definition on people. In other words, the plausibility of this or that conception of what is sexually "normal" depends upon specific social circumstances. When we add up all these factors—social definitions of reality, social relations that take these for granted, as well as the supporting therapies and legitimations—we have the total plausibility structure of the conception in question.

Thus each conception of the world of whatever character or content can be analyzed in terms of its plausibility structure, because it is only as the individual remains within this structure that the conception of the world in question will remain plausible to him. The strength of this plausibility, ranging from unquestioned certitude through firm probability to mere opinion, will be directly dependent upon the strength of the supporting structure. This dynamics pertains irrespective of whether, by some outside observer's criteria of validity, the notions thus made plausible are true or false. The dynamics most definitely pertains to any religious affirmations about the world because these affirmations are, by their very nature, incapable of being supported by our own sense experience and therefore heavily dependent upon social support.

Each plausibility structure can be further analyzed in terms of its constituent elements—the specific human beings that "inhabit" it, the conversational network by which these "inhabitants" keep the reality in question going, the therapeutic practices and rituals, and the legitimations that go with them. For example, the maintenance of the Catholic faith in the consciousness of the individual requires that he maintain his relationship to the plausibility structure of Catholicism. This is, above all, a community of Catholics in his social milieu who continually support this faith. It will be useful if those who are of the greatest emotional significance to the individual (the ones whom George Herbert Mead called significant others) belong to this supportive community—it does not matter much if, say, the individual's dentist is a non-Catholic, but his wife and his closest personal friends had better be. Within this supportive community there will then be an ongoing conversation that, explicitly and implicitly, keeps a Catholic world going. Explicitly, there is affirmation, confirmation, reiteration of Catholic notions about reality. But there is also an implicit Catholicism in such a community. After all, in everyday life it is just as important that some things can silently be taken for granted as that some things are reaffirmed in so many words. Indeed, the most fundamental assumptions about the world are commonly affirmed by implication—they are so "obvious" that there is no need to put them into words. Our individual, then, operates within what may be called a specifically Catholic conversational apparatus, which, in innumerable ways, each day confirms the Catholic world that he coinhabits with his significant others. If all these social mechanisms function properly, his Catholicism will be as "natural" to him as the color of his hair or his belief in the law of gravity. He will, indeed, be the happy possessor of an *anima naturaliter christiana*, a "naturally Christian soul."

Such flawlessness in the plausibility structure is unlikely. For this reason, the supportive community (in this instance, the institutional church) provides specific practices, rituals, and legitimations that maintain the faith over and beyond its basic maintenance by a Catholic social milieu. This, of course, includes the whole body of pious practices, from the formal sacraments to the private reassurance rites (such as prayer) recommended to the individual. It also includes the body of knowledge (in the Catholic case, vast in volume and of immense sophistication) that provides explanation and justification for each detail of religious life and belief. And in this instance, of course, there is a staff of highly trained experts as well, who mediate the therapeutic and legitimating machinery to the individual. The details of all of this vary in different circumstances, especially as between a situation in which the plausibility structure is more or less coextensive with the individual's over-all social experience (that is, where Catholics constitute the majority) and a situation in which the plausibility structure exists as a deviant enclave within the individual's larger society (that is, where Catholics are a cognitive minority). But the essential point is that the plausibility of Catholicism hinges upon the availability of these social processes.

It may be objected that this has, in some way, always been known, certainly by Catholic thinkers. One may even say that the formula *extra ecclesiam nulla salus* ("there is no salvation outside the church") expresses the same insight in different language. A moment's reflection will, however, indicate that more is involved than a change of language—and, indeed, most theologians would recoil from a translation of the formula into the proposition "no plausibility without the appropriate plausibility structure." Why? Because the translated version offers an *explanation* of belief that divests the specific case of its uniqueness and authority. The mystery of faith now becomes scientifically graspable, practically repeatable, and generally applicable. The magic disappears as the mechanisms of plausibility generation and plausibility maintenance become transparent. The community of faith is now understandable as a *constructed entity*—it has been constructed in a specific human history, by human beings. Conversely, it can be dismantled or reconstructed by the use of the same mechanisms. Indeed, a would-be founder of a religion can be given a sociological blueprint for the fabrication of the necessary plausibility structure—and this blueprint will contain essentially the same basic elements that have gone into the making of the Catholic community of faith. The formula, once an affirmation of unique authority, thus becomes a general rule. It is applicable to Catholics, Protestants, Theravada Buddhists, Communists, vegetarians, and believers in flying saucers. In other words, the theologian's world has become *one world among many*—a generalization of the problem of relativity that goes considerably beyond the dimensions of the problem as previously posed by historical scholarship. To put it simply: History posits the problem of relativity as *a fact*, the sociology of knowledge as *a necessity of our condition*.

If my purpose here were to upset theologians, this point could be elaborated at great length. Since my purpose is to comfort them, I will simply hope that the point has been made sufficiently clear, that enough has been said to justify the suspicion that sociology is the dismal science par excellence of our time, an intrinsically debunking discipline that should be most congenial to nihilists, cynics, and other fit subjects for police surveillance. Both theological and political conservatives have long suspected just this, and their aversion to sociology is based on a sound instinct for survival. I am not interested at the moment in pursuing the question of whether sociology should, in a well-run society, be forbidden as a corruption of the young and as inimical to good order (Plato, I'm sure, would have thought so). As far as the challenge to theological thought is concerned, however, there are unexpected redeeming features to the sociologist's dismal revelations, and it is these that concern me in the present undertaking.

One cannot throw a sop to the dragon of relativity and then go about one's intellectual business as usual, although Max Scheler, the founder of the sociology of knowledge, tried to do just that. In the sphere of theological thought a similar effort has been made in the distinction, particularly dear to the neo-orthodox camp, between "religion" and "Christian faith"[23]: "Religion" falls under all the relativizing categories that anybody can think up, while "Christian faith" is supposed to be somehow immune from all this, because it is a gift of God's grace rather than a product of man and therefore provides a firm ground from which to survey the quicksands of relativity. One of the most ingenious presentations of this approach can be found in Karl Barth's introduction to Feuerbach.[24] Variations of it lie in such distinctions as the one between "profane history" and "salvation history" (long a cherished Protestant dichotomy), or, more recently, between *Historie* and *Geschichte* (a legerdemain of the Bultmann school that, alas, loses much of its persuasiveness in any language but German).

"Profane history" refers to the ordinary course of events, as it can be studied by the historian; "sacred history" is the story of God's acts in the world, which can be grasped only in the perspective of faith. *Historie* refers to actual historical events, while *Geschichte* refers to occurrences in the existence of the believing individual for which the historical events serve as some sort of symbol. For instance, the historian may find out all sorts of things about Jesus of Nazareth. All these historical findings, however, are supposed to be finally irrelevant, because only faith can grasp that this Jesus is Christ, or because the really important thing is not the historical Jesus but the Christ experienced in the existence of the believing Christian. The reason why this sort of reasoning won't do is twofold: First, the differentiation is meaningless to the empirical investigator—"Christian faith" is simply another variant of the phenomenon "religion," "salvation history" of the historical phenomenon as such, and so forth. The differentiation presupposes a prior exit from the empirical sphere, and therefore it cannot be used to solve a problem arising within that sphere. Second, the firm ground is given by God, "by grace alone," and not achievable by man, which leaves us singularly unedified if we are not already convinced we are standing on this ground, for then, inevitably, we must ask for directions on how to get there. Such directions are not forthcoming in this theological approach, and cannot be by its very logic. This kind of effort to solve the problem of relativity curiously repeats the old Calvinist doctrine of election—you don't get there unless you start from there. It follows that those of us who are lacking in this particular sense of election must either resign ourselves to intellectual damnation or look for another method.

Any such method will have to include a willingness to see the relativity business through to its very end. This means giving up any *a priori* immunity claims (be it in the aforementioned neo-orthodox sense, or in the older liberal manner of trying to allow the relativizing dragon "thus far, but no farther"). It seems, however, that when the operation is completed a rather strange thing happens. When everything has been subsumed under the relativizing categories in question (those of history, of the sociology of knowledge, or what-have-you), the question of truth reasserts itself in almost pristine simplicity. Once we know that all human affirmations are subject to scientifically graspable socio-historical processes, *which affirmations are true and which are false?* We cannot avoid the question any more than we can return to the innocence of its pre-relativizing asking. This loss of innocence, however, makes for the difference between asking the question before and after we have passed through the "fiery brook."

The point can be illustrated by examining recent "radical" or "secular" theology, which takes as both its starting point and its final criterion the alleged consciousness of modern man. It then proceeds to relativize religious tradition by assigning it, in part or as a whole, to a consciousness that is now passé, "no longer possible to us," and to translate it, partially or wholly, into terms that are supposedly consonant with the alleged modern consciousness. An important example of this is Rudolf Bultmann's "demythologization" program, which begins with the premise that no one who uses electricity and listens to the radio can any longer believe in the miracle world of the New Testament and ends by translating key elements of the Christian tradition into the categories of existentialism. Essentially the same procedure characterizes all theologians of this tendency, though they vary in method (some, for instance, preferring linguistic philosophy or Jungian psychology to existentialism).

I am not concerned for the moment with either the viability of the translation process or the empirical validity of the premise about modern man, but rather with a hidden *double standard*, which can be put quite simply: The *past*, out of which the tradition comes, is relativized in terms of this or that socio-historical analysis. The *present*, however, remains strangely immune from relativization. In other words, the New Testament writers are seen as afflicted with a false consciousness rooted in their time, but the contemporary analyst takes the consciousness of *his* time as an unmixed intellectual blessing. The electricity- and radio-users are placed intellectually above the Apostle Paul.

This is rather funny. More importantly, in the perspective of the sociology of knowledge, it is an extraordinarily one-sided way of looking at things. What was good for the first century is good for the twentieth. The world view of the New Testament writers was constructed and maintained by the same kind of social processes that construct and maintain the world view of contemporary "radical" theologians. Each has its appropriate plausibility structure, its plausibility-maintaining mechanisms. If this is understood, then the appeal to *any* alleged modern consciousness loses most of its persuasiveness—unless, of course, one can bring oneself to believe that modern consciousness is indeed the embodiment of superior cognitive powers. Some people can manage this with respect to modern philosophers or psychologists. It is hard to carry off such a feat of faith with respect to the average consumer of electricity and modern *Weltanschauung*. One has the terrible suspicion that the Apostle Paul may have been one-up cognitively, after all. As a result of such considerations an important shift takes place in the argument on the alleged demise of the supernatural in contemporary society. The empirical presuppositions of the argument can be left intact. In other words, it may be conceded that there is in the modern world a certain type of consciousness that has difficulties with the supernatural. The statement remains, however, on the level of socio-historical diagnosis. The diagnosed condition is *not* thereupon elevated to the status of an absolute criterion; the contemporary situation is not immune to relativizing analysis. We may say that contemporary consciousness is such and such; we are left with the question of whether we will assent to it. We may agree, say, that contemporary consciousness is incapable of conceiving of either angels or demons. We are still left with the question of whether, possibly, both angels and demons go on existing despite this incapacity of our contemporaries to conceive of them.

One (perhaps literally) redeeming feature of sociological perspective is that relativizing analysis, in being pushed to its final consequence, bends back upon itself. The relativizers are relativized, the debunkers are debunked—indeed, relativization itself is somehow liquidated. What follows is *not*, as some of the early sociologists of knowledge feared, a total paralysis of thought. Rather, it is a new freedom and flexibility in asking questions of truth.

As far as the contemporary religious crisis is concerned, the sociology of knowledge can go further than stating this general principle. It can throw light on the causes of the credibility crisis of religion today; that is, it can relativize the relativizers in much more specific terms, by showing up the salient features of *their* plausibility structure. The most important feature to grasp here is that of modern *pluralism*, by which I mean, in this context, any situation in which there is more than one world view available to the members of a society, that is, a situation in which there is competition between world views.[25]

As I have tried to show, world views remain firmly anchored in subjective certainty to the degree that they are supported by consistent and continuous plausibility structures. In the case of optimal consistency and continuity, they attain the character of unquestioned and unquestionable cer-

titudes. Societies vary in their capacity to provide such firm
plausibility structures. As a general rule of thumb, one can
say that the capacity steadily diminishes as one gets closer to
modern industrial societies. A primitive tribe does much better than an ancient city. The latter, however, is still far better
equipped to produce certitudes than our own social forma-
tions. Modern societies are, by their very nature, highly differentiated and segmented, while at the same time allowing
for a very high degree of communication between their segmented subsocieties. The reasons for this, while complex, are
not at all mysterious. They result from the degree of division
of labor brought about by industrial forms of production,
and from the patterns of settlement, social stratification, and
communication engendered by industrialism. The individual
experiences these patterns in terms of differentiated and segmented processes of socialization, which in most cases begin
in early childhood. As he grows older he finds he must play
many different roles, sometimes quite discrepant ones, and
must segregate some of these roles from each other, since
they are not all equally appropriate to the different parts of
his social life. And, as a result of all this, he comes to maintain an inner detachment or distance with regard to some of
these roles—that is, he plays some of them tongue in cheek.
For example, in his family he is forced to conform to the
manners and morals of middle-class life, while in the company of his contemporaries he is pressured to disregard these
"square" characteristics. As long as he associates with both his
family and his contemporaries, he will then play highly discrepant roles at different times. If he identifies his "real" self
with his family, he will "only superficially" conform to the
mores of his contemporaries; if, as is more likely, he more
fully identifies with the latter, he will "only play along" with
his family. In either case there will be some roles that are
performed tongue in cheek, "insincerely," "superficially"—that
is, with inner detachment.
   Inevitably, this leads to a situation in which most plausibility structures are partial and therefore tenuous. They organize only a part of the individual's world and lack the
compelling character of structures taken to be "natural," inevitable, self-evident. Most individuals in primitive or archaic

societies lived in social institutions (such as tribe, clan, or even polis) that embraced just about all the significant relationships they had with other people. The modern individual exists in a plurality of worlds, migrating back and forth between competing and often contradictory plausibility structures, each of which is weakened by the simple fact of its involuntary coexistence with other plausibility structures. In addition to the reality-confirming significant others, there are always and everywhere "those others," annoying disconfirmers, disbelievers—perhaps the modern nuisance par excellence.

This pluralization of socially available worlds has been of particular importance for religion, again for far from mysterious reasons, the most decisive being the Protestant Reformation and its subsidiary schisms. It is this pluralization, rather than some mysterious intellectual fall from grace, that I see as the most important cause of the diminishing plausibility of religious traditions. It is relatively easy, sociologically speaking, to be a Catholic in a social situation where one can readily limit one's significant others to fellow Catholics, where indeed one has little choice in the matter, and where all the major institutional forces are geared to support and confirm a Catholic world. The story is quite different in a situation where one is compelled to rub shoulders day by day with every conceivable variety of "those others," is bombarded with communications that deny or ignore one's Catholic ideas, and where one has a terrible time even finding some quiet Catholic corners to withdraw into. It is very, very difficult to be cognitively *entre nous* in modern society, especially in the area of religion. This simple sociological fact, and not some magical inexorability of a "scientific" world outlook, is at the basis of the religious plausibility crisis.

The same fact goes far to explain why it is "no longer possible" to believe in the miracles of the New Testament, or in much of anything religiously. Religious affirmations percolate from the level of taken-for-granted certainty to the level of mere belief, opinion, or (a term that eloquently expresses what goes on here) "religious preference." The pluralistic situation not only allows the individual a choice, it forces him to choose. By the same token, it makes religious certainty very hard to come by. It is instructive to recall that the literal meaning of the word *haeresis* is "choice." In a very real sense, every religious community in the pluralistic situation becomes a "heresy," with all the social and psychological tenuousness that the term suggests. In other words, the contemporary radio-user is not inhibited in his capacity for faith by the scientific knowledge and technology that produced his radio. Very likely, he hasn't the first idea of these, and couldn't care less. But he is inhibited by the multiplicity of ideas and notions about the world that his radio, along with other communications media, plunges him into. And while we may understand and sympathize with his predicament, there is no reason whatever to stand in awe of it.

In short, the perspective of sociology, particularly of the sociology of knowledge, can have a definitely liberating effect. While other analytic disciplines free us from the dead weight of the past, sociology frees us from the tyranny of the present. Once we grasp our own situation in sociological terms, it ceases to impress us as an inexorable fate. Of course, we still cannot magically jump out of our own skins. The forces of our situation work on us even if we understand them, because we are social beings and continue to be even when we become sociologists. But we gain at least a measure of liberation from the taken-for-granted certitudes of our time. The German historian Ranke said that "each age is immediate to God," intending thereby to reject the vulgar progressivism that sees one's own moment in history as history's pinnacle. The perspective of sociology increases our ability to investigate whatever truth each age may have discovered in its particular "immediacy to God."

While this, I think, is a considerable intellectual gain, I would like to go further, to suggest that the entire view of religion as a human product or projection may once again be inverted, and that in such an inversion lies a viable theological method in response to the challenge of sociology. If I am right in this, what could be in the making here is a gigantic joke on Feuerbach.

Feuerbach regarded religion as a gigantic projection of man's own being, that is, as essentially man writ large. He therefore proposed reducing theology to anthropology, that is, explaining religion in terms of its underlying human reality. In doing this, Feuerbach took over Hegel's notion of dialectics, but profoundly changed its significance. The concept of dialectics, in Hegel as elsewhere, refers to a reciprocal relation between a subject and its object, a "conversation" between consciousness and whatever is outside consciousness. Hegel's notion of this was first developed in a theological context, the "conversation" was ultimately one between man and God. With Feuerbach, it was a "conversation" between man and man's own productions. Put differently, instead of a dialogue between man and a superhuman reality, religion became a sort of human monologue.

A good case could be made that not only Marx's and Freud's treatment of religion, but the entire historical-psychological-sociological analysis of religious phenomena since Feuerbach has been primarily a vast elaboration of the same conception and the same procedure. A sociological theory of religion, particularly if it is undertaken in the framework of the sociology of knowledge, pushes to its final consequences the Feuerbachian notion of religion as a human projection, that is, as a scientifically graspable producer of human history.[26]

It is relevant to keep in mind that Feuerbach, Marx, and Freud all inverted the original Hegelian dialectic. Their opponents regarded the inversion as standing the dialectic on its head, while their protagonists conceived of it as putting the dialectic back on its feet. The choice of image obviously depends on one's ultimate assumptions about reality. It is logically possible, however, that *both* perspectives may coexist, each within its particular frame of reference. What appears as a human projection in one may appear as a reflection of divine realities in another. The logic of the first perspective does not preclude the possibility of the latter.

An analogy may be useful in illustrating this point. If there is any intellectual enterprise that appears to be a pure projection of human consciousness it is mathematics. A mathematician can be totally isolated from any contact with nature and still go on about his business of constructing mathematical universes, which spring from his mind as pure creations of human intellect. Yet the most astounding result of modern natural science is the reiterated discovery (quite apart from this or that mathematical formulation of natural processes) that nature, too, is in its essence a fabric of mathematical relations. Put crudely, the mathematics that man projects out of his own consciousness somehow corresponds to a mathematical reality that is external to him, and which indeed his consciousness appears to reflect. How is this possible? It is possible, of course, because man himself is part of the same over-all reality, so that there is a fundamental affinity between the structures of his consciousness and the structures of the empirical world. Projection and reflection are movements within the same encompassing reality.

The same may be true of the projections of man's religious imagination. In any case it would seem that any theological method worthy of the name should be based on this possibility. This most emphatically does *not* mean a search for religious phenomena that will somehow manifest themselves as different from human projections. Nothing is immune to the relativization of socio-historical analysis. Whatever else these phenomena may be, they will *also* be human projections, products of human history, social constructions undertaken by human beings. The meta-empirical cannot be conceived of as a kind of enclave within the empirical world, any more, incidentally, than freedom can be conceived of as a hole in the fabric of causality. The theological decision will have to be that, "in, with, and under" the immense array of human projections, there are indicators of a reality that is truly "other" and that the religious imagination of man ultimately reflects.

These considerations also indicate a possible theological starting point, hardly an exclusive one, but one peculiarly apt to meet the challenge previously outlined. This is the starting point of anthropology, using the term in the continental sense, as referring to the philosophical enterprise that concerns itself with the question "What is man?" If the religious projections of man correspond to a reality that is superhuman and supernatural, then it seems logical to look for traces of this reality in the projector himself. This is not to suggest an empirical theology—that would be logically impossible—but rather a theology of very high empirical sensitivity that seeks to correlate its propositions with what can be empirically known. To the extent that its starting point is anthropological, such a theology will return to some of the fundamental concerns of Protestant liberalism—without, it is to be hoped, the latter's deference to the "cultured despisers of religion" and their assorted utopianisms.

3. Theological Possibilities: Starting with Man

If anthropology is understood here in a very broad sense, as any systematic inquiry into the constitution and condition of man, it will be clear that any kind of theology will have to include an anthropological dimension. After all, theological propositions only very rarely deal with the divine in and of itself, but rather in its relations to and significance for man. Even the most abstract speculations concerning the nature of the Trinity were much more salvation-oriented than theoretical in their underlying impetus, that is, they derived not from disinterested curiosity but from a burning concern for the redemption of man. The real question, then, is not so much whether theology relates to anthropology—it can hardly help doing so—but what kind of relation there will be.

Classical Protestant liberalism in the nineteenth century and up to about World War I was concerned with anthropology because, in one way or another, it sought to derive the truth of the Christian tradition from the data of human history. In line with the mood of this era of a triumphant bourgeois civilization, its anthropology was marked by a profound confidence in the rationality and perfectibility of man as well as by faith in the progressive course of man's history. Not surprisingly, this optimistic stance lost plausibility as the crisis of bourgeois civilization deepened in the wake of World War I. The naïve and situation-bound aspects of the liberal anthropology (in its religious as well as secular forms) became all too apparent. To the extent that neo-orthodox theology uncovered the shallow and utopian sides of liberalism, its protest was undoubtedly justified and even necessary. This, however, does not validate its own anthropological orientation.[27]

One of the key characteristics of the neo-orthodox reaction to theological liberalism was its violent rejection of the latter's historical and anthropological starting points. Liberalism had emphasized man's ways toward God, neo-orthodoxy emphasized God's dealings with man. No human experience was any longer to serve as the starting point of the theological enterprise, but rather the stark majesty of God's revelation that confronted man as negation, judgment, and grace. Neo-orthodoxy dared to pronounce once more a *Deus dixit*—"Thus saith the Lord."

In a very real sense neo-orthodoxy, in its original impulse, was anti-anthropological. There were to be no approaches from men to God, only the one approach from God to man, by means of a divine revelation that was due wholly to God's activity and not in any way rooted in man's nature or condition. Any anthropological statements (such as statements about man's sinfulness) could be made only in terms of this revelation. In other words, an anthropology could be theologically deduced, but there were no inductive possibilities *from* anthropology *to* theology. This orientation was, of course, sharpest in the early work of Karl Barth with its radical return to the God-centered and revelation-based thought of the Protestant Reformation. It is in this context that one can understand Barth's view that the decisive dividing line between Protestantism and Catholicism is the attitude toward the notion of *analogia entis* (the scholastic conception of an "analogy of being" between God and man)—Protestantism, according to Barth, had to pronounce a resounding "no!" to this notion.

The starkness of this position was too much even for many within the neo-orthodox movement. In the 1930s it was another Swiss theologian, Emil Brunner, in his controversy with Barth, who most clearly represented the modification of the neo-orthodox aversion to anthropological considerations. Significantly, Brunner was greatly interested in what he called the problem of the *Anknüpfungspunkt*—the "point of contact" between God's revelation and the human situation. This interest, largely fostered by practical considerations of evan-

gelism and pastoral care, reintroduced anthropological perspectives into the neo-orthodox position. But now, quite
logically, the anthropological propositions picked up by theologians tended to be those that stressed the "lostness" and
misery of the human condition. The worse the picture of
man, the greater the chance to make credible (*anknüpfen*)
the claims of revelation. The gloomy anthropology of existentialism was amply suited to this purpose.

Later, particularly in America, the more pessimistic ver-
sions of Freudian anthropology were added. Thus concepts
such as despair, *Angst*, "thrown-ness" became stock-in-trade
terms of neo-orthodox theologians. For a while it seemed that
the necessary counterpoint of the Christian proclamation was
an anthropology of desperation—man, the object of the proclamation, was a murderous, incestuous figure, sunk in utter
misery, without any hope except the hope of grace offered by
God's revelation.

Needless to say, such an anthropology had a good deal to
recommend itself during the twelve apocalyptic years between
1933 and 1945, and for some years after that. But even then
there were some who were uneasy about the one-sidedness
and even some who, with Albert Camus, came to feel that
"in a time of pestilence" we learn "that there are more things
to admire in men than to despise."[28]

The celebration of secularity that came to the fore in the
theology of more recent years, of which John Robinson's *Honest to God* (1963) and Harvey Cox's *The Secular City*
(1965) were popular high points, naturally turned to more
cheerful anthropological perspectives. The moral mood came
closer to an endorsement of "enjoy, enjoy!" than to the earlier
recommendation to be as anxious as possible. The social world
was once more seen as an arena of purposeful action for human betterment rather than as a quagmire of futilities. And
this, again, had strong roots in the general intellectual trends
of the time. After all, even Jean-Paul Sartre turned from his
fascination with the alleged impossibility of love to a commitment to world-transforming revolutionary action. Such an optimistic reversal would appear to be a necessary condition for
the secularization of Christianity. The secularizing theologian
wishes to translate the tradition into terms that are immanent

to "this eon." If such an undertaking is to have minimal attractiveness, "this eon" had better be worth the effort. Logically enough, notions such as "autonomy," "man come of age,"
and even "democratic humanism" came to be substituted for
the earlier expressions of existential anguish. Indeed, if one
looks at all this with a little detachment, one is strongly reminded of the children's game of rapidly changing grimaces—
"now I'm crying"/"now I'm laughing"—only children don't
construct a philosophy to go with each phase of the game.

Enough has been said earlier to indicate that, captive
though we all are of the circumstances in which our thinking
must take place, what is being suggested here is at least a
measure of emancipation from this sequence of "mood theologies." The suggestion that theological thought revert to an
anthropological starting point is motivated by the belief that
such an anchorage in fundamental human experience might
offer some protection against the constantly changing winds
of cultural moods. In other words, I am not proposing a "more
relevant" program or a new dating of our intellectual situation
("post-X" or "neo-Y"). Instead, I venture to hope that there
may be theological possibilities whose life span is at least a
little longer than the duration of any one cultural or sociopolitical crisis of the times.

What could an anthropological starting point mean for theology?

I am not in a position to answer this question by systematically confronting the vast literature that has accumulated in
philosophical anthropology in recent decades. Nor can I present the design for a theological system that might emerge
from this starting point. Such achievements must be left to
professional philosophers and professional theologians (or
perhaps, who knows, to teams that combine both types of expertise). But it is very unsatisfactory simply to produce assignments for other people. Very modestly then and with full
awareness of my all too obvious limitations, let me give a few
indications of the direction in which I think it is possible to
move.

I would suggest that theological thought seek out what
might be called *signals of transcendence* within the empirically given human situation. And I would further suggest that

there are *prototypical human gestures* that may constitute such signals. What does this mean?

By signals of transcendence I mean phenomena that are to be found within the domain of our "natural" reality but that appear to point beyond that reality. In other words, I am not using transcendence here in a technical philosophical sense but literally, as the transcending of the normal, everyday world that I earlier identified with the notion of the "supernatural." By prototypical human gestures I mean certain reiterated acts and experiences that appear to express essential aspects of man's being, of the human animal as such. I do *not* mean what Jung called "archetypes"—potent symbols buried deep in the unconscious mind that are common to all men. The phenomena I am discussing are not "unconscious" and do not have to be excavated from the "depths" of the mind; they belong to ordinary everyday awareness.

One fundamental human trait, which is of crucial importance in understanding man's religious enterprise, is his propensity for order.[29] As the philosopher of history Eric Voegelin points out at the beginning of *Order and History*, his analysis of the various human conceptions of order: "The order of history emerges from the history of order. Every society is burdened with the task, under its concrete conditions, of creating an order that will endow the fact of its existence with meaning in terms of ends divine and human."[30] Any historical society is an order, a protective structure of meaning, erected in the face of chaos. Within this order the life of the group as well as the life of the individual makes sense. Deprived of such order, both group and individual are threatened with the most fundamental terror, the terror of chaos that Emile Durkheim called *anomie* (literally, a state of being "order-less").

Throughout most of human history men have believed that the created order of society, in one way or another, corresponds to an underlying order of the universe, a divine order that supports and justifies all human attempts at ordering. Now, clearly, not every such belief in correspondence can be true, and a philosophy of history may, like Voegelin's, be an inquiry into the relationship of true order to the different human attempts at ordering. But there is a more basic element to be considered, over and above the justification of this or that historically produced order. This is the human faith in order as such, a faith closely related to man's fundamental trust in reality. This faith is experienced not only in the history of societies and civilizations, but in the life of each individual—indeed, child psychologists tell us there can be no maturation without the presence of this faith at the outset of the socialization process. Man's propensity for order is grounded in a faith or trust that, ultimately, reality is "in order," "all right," "as it should be." Needless to say, there is no empirical method by which this faith can be tested. To assert it is itself an act of faith. But it is possible to proceed from the faith that is rooted in experience to the act of faith that transcends the empirical sphere, a procedure that could be called the *argument from ordering*.

In this fundamental sense, every ordering gesture is a signal of transcendence. This is certainly the case with the great ordering gestures that the historian of religion Mircea Eliade called "nomizations"—such as the archaic ceremonies in which a certain territory was solemnly incorporated into a society, or the celebration, in our own culture as in older ones, of the setting up of a new household through the marriage of two individuals. But it is equally true of more everyday occurrences. Consider the most ordinary, and probably most fundamental, of all—the ordering gesture by which a mother reassures her anxious child.

A child wakes up in the night, perhaps from a bad dream, and finds himself surrounded by darkness, alone, beset by nameless threats. At such a moment the contours of trusted reality are blurred or invisible, and in the terror of incipient chaos the child cries out for his mother. It is hardly an exaggeration to say that, at this moment, the mother is being invoked as a high priestess of protective order. It is she (and, in many cases, she alone) who has the power to banish the chaos and to restore the benign shape of the world. And, of course, any good mother will do just that. She will take the child and cradle him in the timeless gesture of the Magna Mater who became our Madonna. She will turn on a lamp, perhaps, which will encircle the scene with a warm glow of reassuring light. She will speak or sing to the child, and the

content of this communication will invariably be the same
—"Don't be afraid—everything is in order, everything is all
right." If all goes well, the child will be reassured, his trust in
reality recovered, and in this trust he will return to sleep.

All this, of course, belongs to the most routine experiences
of life and does not depend upon any religious preconcep-
tions. Yet this common scene raises a far from ordinary question, which immediately introduces a religious dimension: *Is
the mother lying to the child?* The answer, in the most profound sense, can be "no" only if there is some truth in the
religious interpretation of human existence. Conversely, if the
"natural" is the only reality there is, the mother is lying to the
child—lying out of love, to be sure, and obviously *not* lying
to the extent that her reassurance is grounded in the fact of
this love—but, in the final analysis, lying all the same. Why?
*Because the reassurance, transcending the immediately pres-
ent two individuals and their situation, implies a statement
about reality as such.*

To become a parent is to take on the role of world-builder
and world-protector. This is so, of course, in the obvious sense
that parents provide the environment in which a child's socialization takes place and serve as mediators to the child of
the entire world of the particular society in question. But it
is also so in a less obvious, more profound sense, which is
brought out in the scene just described. The role that a parent
takes on represents not only the order of this or that society,
but order as such, the underlying order of the universe that it
makes sense to trust. It is this role that may be called the role
of high priestess. It is a role that the mother in this scene
plays willy-nilly, regardless of her own awareness or (more
likely) lack of awareness of just what it is she is representing.
"*Everything* is in order, *everything* is all right"—this is the
basic formula of maternal and parental reassurance. Not just
this particular anxiety, not just this particular pain—but
everything is all right. The formula can, without in any way
violating it, be translated into a statement of cosmic scope—
"Have trust in being." This is precisely what the formula intrinsically implies. And if we are to believe the child psychologists (which we have good reason to do in this instance),
this is an experience that is absolutely essential to the process

of becoming a human person. Put differently, at the very center of the process of becoming fully human, at the core of
humanitas, we find an experience of trust in the order of
reality. Is this experience an illusion? Is the individual who
represents it a liar?

If reality is coextensive with the "natural" reality that our
empirical reason can grasp, then the experience *is* an illusion
and the role that embodies it *is* a lie. For then it is perfectly
obvious that everything is *not* in order, is *not* all right. The
world that the child is being told to trust is the same world
in which he will eventually die. If there is no other world,
then the ultimate truth about this one is that eventually it
will kill the child as it will kill his mother. This would not,
to be sure, detract from the real presence of love and its
very real comforts; it would even give this love a quality of
tragic heroism. Nevertheless, the final truth would be not
love but terror, not light but darkness. The nightmare of
chaos, not the transitory safety of order, would be the final
reality of the human situation. For, in the end, we must all
find ourselves in darkness, alone with the night that will swal-
low us up. The face of reassuring love, bending over our terror, will then be nothing except an image of merciful illusion.
In that case the last word about religion is Freud's. Religion
is the childish fantasy that our parents run the universe for
our benefit, a fantasy from which the mature individual must
free himself in order to attain whatever measure of stoic resignation he is capable of.

It goes without saying that the preceding argument is not
a moral one. It does not condemn the mother for this charade
of world-building, if it be a charade. It does not dispute the
right of atheists to be parents (though it is not without interest that there have been atheists who have rejected parent-
hood for exactly these reasons). The argument from ordering
is metaphysical rather than ethical. To restate it: In the observable human propensity to order reality there is an intrinsic impulse to give cosmic scope to this order, an impulse
that implies not only that human order in some way corresponds to an order that transcends it, but that this transcendent order is of such a character that man can trust himself
and his destiny to it. There is a variety of human roles that

represent this conception of order, but the most fundamental is the parental role. Every parent (or, at any rate, every parent who loves his child) takes upon himself the representation of a universe that is ultimately in order and ultimately trustworthy. This representation can be justified only within a religious (strictly speaking a supernatural) frame of reference. In this frame of reference the natural world within which we are born, love, and die is not the only world, but only the foreground of another world in which love is not annihilated in death, and in which, therefore, the trust in the power of love to banish chaos is justified. Thus man's ordering propensity implies a transcendent order, and each ordering gesture is a signal of this transcendence. The parental role is not based on a loving lie. On the contrary, it is a witness to the ultimate truth of man's situation in reality. In that case, it is perfectly possible (even, if one is so inclined, in Freudian terms) to analyze religion as a cosmic projection of the child's experience of the protective order of parental love. What is projected is, however, itself a reflection, an imitation, of ultimate reality. Religion, then, is not only (from the point of view of empirical reason) a projection of human order, but (from the point of view of what might be called *inductive faith*) the ultimately true vindication of human order.

Since the term "inductive faith" will appear a number of times, its meaning should be clarified. I use induction to mean any process of thought that begins with experience. Deduction is the reverse process; it begins with ideas that precede experience. By "inductive faith," then, I mean a religious process of thought that begins with facts of human experience; conversely, "deductive faith" begins with certain assumptions (notably assumptions about divine revelation) that cannot be tested by experience. Put simply, inductive faith moves from human experience to statements about God, deductive faith from statements about God to interpretations of human experience.

Closely related to, though still distinct from, the foregoing considerations is what I will call the *argument from play*. Once more, as the Dutch historian Johan Huizinga has shown, we are dealing with a basic experience of man.[31] Ludic, or playful, elements can be found in just about any sector of human culture, to the point where it can be argued that culture as such would be impossible without this dimension. One aspect of play that Huizinga analyzes in some detail is the fact that play sets up a separate universe of discourse, with its own rules, which suspends, "for the duration," the rules and general assumptions of the "serious" world. One of the most important assumptions thus suspended is the time structure of ordinary social life. When one is playing, one is on a different time, no longer measured by the standard units of the larger society, but rather by the peculiar ones of the game in question. In the "serious" world it may be 11 A.M., on such and such a day, month, and year. But in the universe in which one is playing it may be the third round, the fourth act, the *allegro* movement, or the second kiss. In playing, one steps out of one time into another.[32]

This is true of all play. Play always constructs an enclave within the "serious" world of everyday social life, and an enclave within the latter's chronology as well. This is also true of play that creates pain rather than joy. It may be 11 A.M., say, but in the universe of the torturer it will be thumbscrews time again. Nevertheless one of the most pervasive features of play is that it is usually a joyful activity. Indeed, when it ceases to be joyful and becomes misery or even indifferent routine, we tend to think of this as a perversion of its intrinsic character. Joy is play's intention. When this intention is actually realized, in joyful play, the time structure of the playful universe takes on a very specific quality— namely, *it becomes eternity*. This is probably true of all experiences of intense joy, even when they are not enveloped in the separate reality of play. This is the final insight of Nietzsche's Zarathustra in the midnight song: "All joy wills eternity—wills deep, deep eternity!"[33] This intention is, however, particularly patent in the joy experienced in play, precisely because the playful universe has a temporal dimension that is more than momentary and that can be perceived as a distinct structure. In other words, in joyful play it appears as if one were stepping not only from one chronology into another, but from time into eternity. Even as one remains conscious of the poignant reality of that other, "serious" time in which one is moving toward death, one apprehends joy as

being, in some barely conceivable way, a joy forever. Joyful
play appears to suspend, or bracket, the reality of our "living
towards death" (as Heidegger aptly described our "serious"
condition).

It is this curious quality, which belongs to all joyful play,
that explains the liberation and peace such play provides. In
early childhood, of course, the suspension is unconscious,
since there is as yet no consciousness of death. In later life
play brings about a beatific reiteration of childhood. When
adults play with genuine joy, they momentarily regain the
deathlessness of childhood. This becomes most apparent
when such play occurs in the actual face of acute suffering
and dying. It is this that stirs us about men making music in
a city under bombardment or a man doing mathematics on
his deathbed. C. S. Lewis, in a sermon preached at the beginning of World War II, put this eloquently: "Human life
has always been lived on the edge of a precipice. . . . Men
. . . propound mathematical theorems in beleaguered cities,
conduct metaphysical arguments in condemned cells, make
jokes on scaffolds, discuss the last new poem while advancing
to the walls of Quebec, and comb their hair at Thermopylae.
This is not *panache*: it is our nature."[84] It is our nature because, as Huizinga suggests, man is profoundly *homo ludens*.
It is his ludic constitution that allows man, even at Thermopylae, to regain and ecstatically realize the deathless joy of his
childhood.

Some little girls are playing hopscotch in the park. They
are completely intent on their game, closed to the world outside it, happy in their concentration. Time has stood still
for them—or, more accurately, it has been collapsed into the
movements of the game. The outside world has, for the duration of the game, ceased to exist. And, by implication (since
the little girls may not be very conscious of this), pain and
death, which are the law of that world, have also ceased to
exist. Even the adult observer of this scene, who is perhaps all
too conscious of pain and death, is momentarily drawn into
the beatific immunity.

In the playing of adults, at least on certain occasions, the
suspension of time and of the "serious" world in which people suffer and die becomes explicit. Just before the Soviet

troops occupied Vienna in 1945, the Vienna Philharmonic gave one of its scheduled concerts. There was fighting in the immediate proximity of the city, and the concertgoers could hear the rumbling of the guns in the distance. The entry of the Soviet army interrupted the concert schedule—if I'm not mistaken, for about a week. Then the concerts resumed, as scheduled. In the universe of this particular play, the world-shattering events of the Soviet invasion, the overthrow of one empire and the cataclysmic appearance of another, meant a small interruption in the program. Was this simply a case of callousness, of indifference to suffering? Perhaps in the case of some individuals, but, basically, I would say not. It was rather an affirmation of the ultimate triumph of all human gestures of creative beauty over the gestures of destruction, and even over the ugliness of war and death.

The logic of the argument from play is very similar to that of the argument from order. The experience of joyful play is not something that must be sought on some mystical margin of existence. It can be readily found in the reality of ordinary life. Yet within this experienced reality it constitutes a signal of transcendence, because its intrinsic intention points beyond itself and beyond man's "nature" to a "supernatural" justification. Again, it will be perfectly clear that this justification cannot be empirically proved. Indeed, the experience can be plausibly interpreted as a merciful illusion, a regression to childish magic (along the lines, say, of the Freudian theory of wishful fantasy). The religious justification of the experience can be achieved only in an act of faith. The point, however, is that this faith is inductive—it does not rest on a mysterious revelation, but rather on what we experience in our common, ordinary lives. All men have experienced the deathlessness of childhood and we may assume that, even if only once or twice, all men have experienced transcendent joy in adulthood. Under the aspect of inductive faith, religion is the final vindication of childhood and of joy, and of all gestures that replicate these.

Another essential element of the human situation is hope, and there is an *argument from hope* within the same logic of inductive faith. In recent philosophical anthropology, this element has been particularly emphasized by the French phi-

losopher Gabriel Marcel (in the context of a Christian existentialism) and by the German philosopher Ernst Bloch (in
a Marxist context). A number of theologians, influenced
by Bloch, have taken up this theme in their dialogue with
Marxism.[85]

Bloch emphasizes that man's being cannot be adequately
understood except in connection with man's unconquerable
propensity to hope for the future. As a Marxist, Bloch, of
course, relates this to the revolutionary hope of transforming
the world for human betterment. Some theologians have argued that such hope is also the essence of Christianity (and,
incidentally, that therefore Christians should not necessarily
be anti-revolutionary). This is not the place to discuss these
developments, though it should be said that the argument
here is compatible with but not directly indebted to them.[86]

Human existence is always oriented toward the future. Man
exists by constantly extending his being into the future, both
in his consciousness and in his activity. Put differently, man
realizes himself in projects. An essential dimension of this
"futurity" of man is hope. It is through hope that men overcome the difficulties of any given here and now. And it is
through hope that men find meaning in the face of extreme
suffering. A key ingredient of most (but not all) theodicies
is hope. The specific content of such hope varies. In earlier
periods of human history, when the concept of the individual
and his unique worth was not as yet so sharply defined, this
hope was commonly invested in the future of the group. The
individual might suffer and die, be defeated in his most important projects, but the group (clan, or tribe, or people)
would live on and eventually triumph. Often, of course, theodicies were based on the hope of an individual afterlife, in
which the sufferings of this earthly life would be vindicated
and left behind. Through most of human history, both collective and individual theodicies of hope were legitimated in
religious terms. Under the impact of secularization, ideologies of this-worldly hope have come to the fore as theodicies
(the Marxist one being the most important of late). In any
case, human hope has always asserted itself most intensely in
the face of experiences that seemed to spell utter defeat,
most intensely of all in the face of the final defeat of death.

Thus the profoundest manifestations of hope are to be found in gestures of courage undertaken in defiance of death.

Courage, of course, can be exhibited by individuals committed to every kind of cause—good, bad, or indifferent. A cause is not justified by the courage of its proponents. After all, there were some very courageous Nazis. The kind of courage I am interested in here is linked to hopes for human creation, justice, or compassion; that is, linked to other gestures of *humanitas*—the artist who, against all odds and even in failing health, strives to finish his creative act; the man who risks his life to defend or save innocent victims of oppression; the man who sacrifices his own interests and comfort to come to the aid of afflicted fellow men. There is no need to belabor the point with examples. Suffice it to say that it is this kind of courage and hope that I have in mind in this argument.

We confront here once more, then, observable phenomena of the human situation whose intrinsic intention appears to be a depreciation or even denial of the reality of death. Once more, under the aspect of inductive faith, these phenomena are signals of transcendence, pointers toward a religious interpretation of the human situation. Psychologists tell us (correctly no doubt) that, though we may fear our own death, we cannot really imagine it. Our innermost being shrinks from the image and even theoretical detachment seems to be caught in this fundamental incapacity. It is partly on this basis that Sartre has criticized Heidegger's concept of "living unto death," arguing that we are fundamentally incapable of such an attitude. The only death we can experience, Sartre maintains, is the death of others; our own death can never be part of our experience, and it eludes even our imagination. Yet it is precisely in the face of the death of others, and especially of others that we love, that our rejection of death asserts itself most loudly. It is here, above all, that everything we are calls out for a hope that will refute the empirical fact. It would seem, then, that both psychologically (in the failure to imagine his own death) and morally (in his violent denial of the death of others) a "no!" to death is profoundly rooted in the very being of man.

This refusal is to be found in more than what Karl Jaspers

called the "marginal situations" of human life—such extreme
experiences as critical illness, war, or other natural or social
catastrophes. There are, of course, trivial expressions of hope
that do not contain this dimension—"I hope that we will have
good weather for our picnic." But any hope that, in whatever
way, involves the individual as a whole already implicitly
contains this ultimate refusal—"I hope to finish my work
as a scientist as well as I can"—"I hope to make a success of
my marriage"—"I hope to be brave when I must speak up
against the majority." All these contain an ultimate refusal to
capitulate before the inevitability of death. After all, even
as I express these limited hopes, I know that I may die before my work is finished, that the woman I marry may even
now be afflicted by a fatal disease, or that some majorities, if
outraged enough, may kill me. The denial of death implicit
in hope becomes more manifest, of course, in the extreme
cases—"I hope to finish my work as well as I can, despite the
war that is about to destroy my city"—"I shall marry this
woman, despite what the doctor has just told me about her
condition"—"I shall say my piece, despite the murderous plans
of my enemies."

It is again very clear that both the psychological and moral
aspects of such denial can be explained within the confines
of empirical reason. Our fear of death is instinctually rooted
and presumably has a biological survival value in the process
of evolution. The psychological paralysis before the thought
of our own death can be plausibly explained in terms of the
combination of the instinctual recoil before death and the
peculiarly human knowledge of its inevitability. The moral
refusal to accept the death of others can equally plausibly
be explained as nothing but a "rationalization" (in the Freudian sense) of instinctual and psychological forces. In this perspective, the denial of death and any manifestation of hope
(religious or otherwise) that embodies this denial is a symptom of "childishness." This, indeed, was the burden of
Freud's analysis of religion. Against such "childish" hopes
there stands the "mature" acceptance of what is taken to be
final reality, an essentially stoic attitude which, in the case of
Freud, Philip Rieff has aptly called the "ethic of honesty."[87]
It hardly needs to be said that this kind of stoicism merits

the deepest respect and, in fact, constitutes one of the most impressive attitudes of which man is capable. Freud's calm courage in the face of Nazi barbarity and in his own final illness may be cited as a prime example of this human achievement.

Nevertheless the twin concepts of "childishness" and "maturity" are based on an a priori metaphysical choice that does not follow of necessity from the facts of the matter. The choice does not even necessarily follow if we are convinced (which, let it be added, I am not) by the Freudian interpretation of the psychological genesis of death-denying hope. Man's "no!" to death—be it in the frantic fear of his own annihilation, in moral outrage at the death of a loved other, or in death-defying acts of courage and self-sacrifice—appears to be an intrinsic constituent of his being. There seems to be a death-refusing hope at the very core of our *humanitas*. While empirical reason indicates that this hope is an illusion, there is something in us that, however shamefacedly in an age of triumphant rationality, goes on saying "no!" and even says "no!" to the ever so plausible explanations of empirical reason.

In a world where man is surrounded by death on all sides, he continues to be a being who says "no!" to death—and through this "no!" is brought to faith in another world, the reality of which would validate his hope as something other than illusion. It is tempting to think here of a kind of Cartesian reduction, in which one finally arrives at a root fact of consciousness that says "no!" to death and "yes!" to hope. In any case, the argument from hope follows the logical direction of induction from what is empirically given. It starts from experience but takes seriously those implications or intentions within experience that transcend it—and takes them, once again, as signals of a transcendent reality.

Inductive faith acknowledges the omnipresence of death (and thus of the futility of hope) in "nature," but it also takes into account the intentions within our "natural" experience of hope that point toward a "supernatural" fulfillment. This reinterpretation of our experience encompasses rather than contradicts the various explanations of empirical reason (be they psychological, sociological, or what-have-you). Religion, in justifying this reinterpretation, is the ultimate vindication of hope and courage, just as it is the ultimate vindication of childhood and joy. By the same token, religion vindicates the gestures in which hope and courage are embodied in human action—including, given certain conditions, the gestures of revolutionary hope and, in the ultimate irony of redemption, the courage of stoic resignation.

A somewhat different sort of reasoning is involved in what I will call the *argument from damnation*. This refers to experiences in which our sense of what is humanly permissible is so fundamentally outraged that the only adequate response to the offense as well as to the offender seems to be a curse of supernatural dimensions. I advisedly choose this negative form of reasoning, as against what may at first appear to be a more obvious argument from a positive sense of justice. The latter argument would, of course, lead into the territory of "natural law" theories, where I am reluctant to go at this point. As is well known, these theories have been particularly challenged by the relativizing insights of both the historian and the social scientist, and while I suspect that these challenges can be met, this is not the place to negotiate the question. The negative form of the argument makes the intrinsic intention of the human sense of justice stand out much more sharply as a signal of transcendence over and beyond socio-historical relativities.

The ethical and legal discussion that surrounded, and still surrounds, the trials of Nazi war criminals has given every thinking person, at least in Western countries, an unhappy opportunity to reflect upon these matters. I will not discuss here either the agonizing question "How can such things have been done by human beings?" or the practical question of how the institution of the law is to deal with evil of this scope. In America both questions have been debated very fruitfully in the wake of the publication of Hannah Arendt's *Eichmann in Jerusalem*, and I do not wish to contribute to the debate here. What concerns me at the moment is not how Eichmann is to be explained or how Eichmann should have been dealt with, but rather *the character and intention of our condemnation* of Eichmann. For here is a case (as Arendt revealed, especially in the last pages of her book) in which condemnation can be posited as an absolute and compelling necessity, irrespective of how the case is explained or of what practical consequences one may wish to draw from it. Indeed, a refusal to condemn in absolute terms would appear to offer prima facie evidence not only of a profound failure in the understanding of justice, but more profoundly of a fatal impairment of *humanitas*.

There are certain deeds that cry out to heaven. These deeds are not only an outrage to our moral sense, they seem to violate a fundamental awareness of the constitution of our humanity. In this way, these deeds are not only evil, but *monstrously evil*. And it is this monstrosity that seems to compel even people normally or professionally given to such perspectives to suspend relativizations. It is one thing to say that moralities are socio-historical products, which are relative in time and space. It is quite another thing to say that *therefore* the deeds of an Eichmann can be viewed with scientific detachment as simply an instance of one such morality —and thus, ultimately, can be considered a matter of taste. Of course, it is possible, and for certain purposes may be very useful, to attempt a dispassionate analysis of the case, but it seems impossible to let the matter rest there. It also seems impossible to say something like, "Well, we may not like this at all, we may be outraged or appalled, but that is only because we come from a certain background and have been socialized into certain values—we would react quite differently if we had been socialized [or, for that matter, resocialized, as Eichmann presumably was] in a different way." To be sure, *within a scientific frame of reference*, such a statement may be quite admissible. The crucial point, though, is that this whole relativizing frame of reference appears woefully inadequate to the phenomenon if it is taken as the last word on the matter. Not only are we constrained to condemn, and to condemn absolutely, but, if we should be in a position to do so, we would feel constrained to take action on the basis of this certainty. The imperative to save a child from murder, even at the cost of killing the putative murderer, appears to be curiously immune to relativizing analysis. It seems impossible to deny it even when, because of cowardice or calculation, it is not obeyed.

The signal of transcendence is to be found in a clarification of this "impossibility." Clearly, the murder of children is both practically and theoretically "possible." It can be done, and has been done in innumerable massacres of the innocent stretching back to the dawn of history. It can also be justified by those who do it, however abhorrent their justifications may seem to others. And it can be explained in a variety of ways by an outside observer. None of these "possibilities," however, touch upon the fundamental "impossibility" that, when everything that can be said about it has been said, still impresses us as the fundamental truth. The transcendent element manifests itself in two steps. First, our condemnation is absolute and certain. It does not permit modification or doubt, and it is made in the conviction that it applies to all times and to all men as well as to the perpetrator or putative perpetrator of the particular deed. In other words, we give the condemnation the status of a necessary and universal truth. But, as sociological analysis shows more clearly than any other, this truth, while empirically given in our situation as men, cannot be empirically demonstrated to be either necessary or universal. We are, then, faced with a quite simple alternative: Either we deny that there is here anything that can be called truth—a choice that would make us deny what we experience most profoundly as our own being; or we must look beyond the realm of our "natural" experience for a validation of our certainty. Second, the condemnation does not seem to exhaust its intrinsic intention in terms of this world alone. Deeds that cry out to heaven also cry out for hell. This is the point that was brought out very clearly in the debate over Eichmann's execution. Without going into the question of either the legality or the wisdom of the execution, it is safe to say that there was a very general feeling that "hanging is not enough" in this case. But what would have been "enough"? If Eichmann, instead of being hanged, had been tortured to death in the most lengthy and cruel manner imaginable, would this have been "enough"? A negative answer seems inevitable. No human punishment is "enough" in the case of deeds as monstrous as these. These are deeds that demand not only condemnation, but *damnation* in the full religious meaning of the word—that is, the doer not only puts himself outside the community of men; he also separates himself in a final way from a moral order that transcends the human community, and thus invokes a retribution that is more than human.

Just as certain gestures can be interpreted as anticipations of redemption, so other gestures can be viewed as anticipations of hell (hell here meaning no more or less than the state of being damned, both here and now and also beyond the confines of this life and this world). We have interpreted the prototypical gesture of a mother holding her child in protective reassurance as a signal of transcendence. A few years ago, a picture was printed that contains the prototypical countergesture. It was taken somewhere in eastern Europe during World War II at a mass execution—of Jews, or of Russians or Poles, nobody seems to know for sure. The picture shows a woman holding a child, supporting it with one hand and with the other pressing its face into her shoulder, and a few feet away a German soldier with raised rifle, taking aim. More recently two pictures have come out of the war in Vietnam that, as it were, separate the components of this paradigm of hell (and, when taken together, serve to remind us that damnation very rarely follows the political dividing lines drawn by men). One picture, taken at an interrogation of "Vietcong suspects," shows an American soldier holding a rifle against the head of a woman of indeterminate age, her face lined with anguish. Whether or not the rifle was eventually fired, the possibility is implied in the threatening gesture. The other picture was taken during the Tet offensive of the Vietcong in early 1968, in a military billet in Saigon where the Vietcong had massacred the families of officers of the South Vietnamese army. It shows an officer carrying his dead daughter in his arms. The lines on his face are like those on the face of the woman being interrogated. Only here we do not see the man with the rifle.

I would argue that both gesture and countergesture imply transcendence, albeit in opposite ways. Both may be understood, under the aspect of inductive faith, as pointing to an ultimate, religious context in human experience. Just as religion vindicates the gesture of protective reassurance, even when it is performed in the face of death, so it also vindicates the ultimate condemnation of the countergesture of inhumanity, precisely because religion provides a context for damnation. Hope and damnation are two aspects of the same, encompassing vindication. The duality, I am inclined to think, is important. To be sure, religious hope offers a theodicy and therefore consolation to the victims of inhumanity. But it is equally significant that religion provides damnation for the perpetrators of inhumanity. The massacre of the innocent (and, in a terrible way, all of history can be seen as this) raises the question of the justice and power of God. It also, however, suggests the necessity of hell—not so much as a confirmation of God's justice, but rather as a vindication of our own.

Finally, there is an *argument from humor*.[38] A good deal has been written about the phenomenon of humor, much of it in a very humorless vein. In recent thought, the two most influential theories on the subject have probably been those of Freud and Bergson.[39] Both interpret humor as the apprehension of a fundamental discrepancy—in Freud's theory, the discrepancy between the demands of superego and libido; in Bergson's, between a living organism and the mechanical world. I have strong reservations about either theory, but I readily concede one common proposition—that the comic (which is the object of any humorous perception) is fundamentally discrepancy, incongruity, incommensurability. This leads to a question, which Freud does not raise because of his psychological perspective and which Bergson, I think, answers incorrectly, as to the nature of the two realities that are discrepant or incongruous with respect to each other.

I agree with Bergson's description: "A situation is invariably comic when it belongs simultaneously to two altogether independent series of events and is capable of being interpreted in two entirely different meanings at the same time."[40] But I insist upon adding that this comic quality always refers to *human* situations, not to encounters between organisms and the non-organic. The biological as such is not comic. Animals become comic only when we view them anthropomorphically, that is, when we imbue them with human characteristics. Within the human sphere, just about any discrepancy can strike us as funny. Discrepancy is the stuff of which jokes are made, and frequently it is the punch line that reveals the "entirely different meaning." The little Jew meets the big Negro. The mouse wants to sleep with the elephant. The great philosopher loses his pants. But I would go further than this and suggest that there is one fundamental discrepancy from which all other comic discrepancies are derived —the discrepancy between man and universe. It is *this* discrepancy that makes the comic an essentially human phenomenon and humor an intrinsically human trait. *The comic reflects the imprisonment of the human spirit in the world.* This is why, as has been pointed out over and over since classical antiquity, comedy and tragedy are at root closely related. Both are commentaries on man's finitude—if one wants to put it in existentialist terms, on his condition of "thrown-ness." If this is so, then the comic is an objective dimension of man's reality, not just a subjective or psychological reaction to that reality. One of the most moving testimonies to this is that made by the French writer David Rousset, commenting on his time spent in a Nazi concentration camp. He writes that one of the few lasting lessons he took with him from this period was the recognition that the comic was an objective fact that was *there* and could be perceived as such, no matter how great the inner terror and anguish of the mind perceiving it.

There is an additional point to be made. Humor not only recognizes the comic discrepancy in the human condition, it also relativizes it, and thereby suggests that the tragic perspective on the discrepancies of the human condition can also be relativized. At least for the duration of the comic perception, the tragedy of man is bracketed. By laughing at the imprisonment of the human spirit, humor implies that this imprisonment is not final but will be overcome, and by this implication provides yet another signal of transcendence— in this instance in the form of an intimation of redemption. I would thus argue that humor, like childhood and play, can be seen as an ultimately religious vindication of joy.

Humor mocks the "serious" business of this world and the mighty who carry it out. There is a story that when Tamerlane conquered Persia he ordered the poet Hafiz to be brought before him and confronted him with one of his poems, in

which he had promised all the glories of Samarkand for the
mole on his sweetheart's cheek. "How dare you offer the
splendor of my imperial capital for the shoddy attractions of
a Persian whore?" Tamerlane angrily demanded. "Your majesty, it is from you that I have learned the habits of generos-
ity," Hafiz is said to have replied. According to the story,
Tamerlane laughed and spared the poet's life. He might well
have reacted differently, conquerors and empire-builders not
usually being endowed with much appreciation for humor.
But whatever the outcome of such encounters between ty-
rants and poets, the question I would always ask is this: Who,
in the end, is to be pitied—the one who holds the world in his
powerful hands, or the one who laughs at him? The "serious"
answer is, of course, that power is not to be pitied, that the
pitiful are always the victims of power. Humor, at least for
the instant in which it perceives the comic dimensions of the
situation, gives the opposite answer. The one to be finally
pitied is the one who has an illusion. And power is the final
illusion, while laughter reveals the final truth. To a degree,
this can be said without any reference to transcendence.
Empirical reason knows that all power is precarious and that
eventually even Tamerlane must die. But the revelation of
laughter points beyond these empirical facts. Power is ultimately an illusion because it cannot transcend the limits of
the empirical world. Laughter can—and does every time it
relativizes the seemingly rocklike necessities of this world.

A prototypical manifestation of the comic in Western literature is the figure of Don Quixote. And a prototypical embodiment of the gestures of humorous liberation is the
clown. Both figures illustrate the basic alternatives in interpreting man's imprisonment in the world. In Cervantes'
novel, the profoundly comic rebellion of Quixote against the
imprisoning walls of the empirical world ends in tragic failure.
At the end, in Alfred Schutz's words, Quixote is "a home-
comer to a world to which he does not belong, enclosed in
everyday reality as in a prison, and tortured by the most
cruel jailer: the common-sense reason which is conscious of
its own limits."[41] No other conclusion is possible from the
point of view of empirical reason. Another conclusion, the
specifically religious one, is eloquently expressed by Enid

Welsford in the last paragraph of her history of the clown as a social and literary figure: "To those who do not repudiate the religious insight of the race, the human spirit is uneasy in this world because it is at home elsewhere, and escape from the prison house is possible not only in fancy but in fact. The theist believes in possible beatitude, because he disbelieves in the dignified isolation of humanity. To him, therefore, romantic comedy is serious literature because it is a foretaste of the truth: the Fool is wiser than the Humanist; and clown-age is less frivolous than the deification of humanity."[42] In a religious frame of reference, it is Quixote's hope rather than Sancho Panza's "realism" that is ultimately vindicated, and the gestures of the clown have a sacramental dignity. Religion reinterprets the meaning of the comic and vindicates laughter.

This is by no means an exhaustive or exclusive list of human gestures that may be seen as signals of transcendence. To provide one would entail constructing a philosophical anthropology and, on top of that, a theological system to go with it. I am not prepared to be quite as Quixotic as that! But I do want to go at least a few steps beyond setting up a program and suggest how it might be possible to theologize from an anthropological starting point. My choice of examples may not be convincing to everyone and, in any case, is fairly arbitrary. I could have chosen other examples, though I would contend that the ones just discussed are particularly useful because they all refer to very basic human experiences. I have deliberately omitted any discussion of claims to direct religious experience (in the sense of experience of the supernatural). This is by no means intended to depreciate efforts to study and understand such phenomena; it merely follows from my earlier expressed belief that theological thought would do well to turn from the projections to the projector, and thus to empirical data about man. It is fairly clear that mysticism, or any other alleged experience of supernatural realities, is not accessible to everyone. Almost by definition, it partakes of the quality of the esoteric. My aim has been to explore theological possibilities that take as their starting point what is generally accessible to all men. I have therefore limited myself to a discussion of phenomena that can be found in everybody's ordinary life. Even the argu-

ment from damnation remains within the context of the
"ordinary," in the sense that it does not presuppose any special illumination or intervention from beyond the human
sphere. I make no claim for this method over any other, but,
to repeat, it is a possible solution to the vertigo of relativity.
It will appeal particularly, I think, to those who have passed
through the "fiery brook" of sociological relativization.

It goes without saying that this procedure raises very complex philosophical questions. Again, I am not prepared to
negotiate them here. But two disclaimers should be made
right away. My procedure does *not* presuppose a static "human nature," somehow outside history. Neither does it presuppose a theory of historical "evolution" or "progress."
There are some prototypical human gestures that appear
timeless and that may be considered as constants in history.
It may be that there are necessary and necessarily recurrent
expressions of *humanitas*. But no one can deny that there
have been far-reaching changes in the understanding of *humanitas* in the course of history. For example, our present
understanding of the relationship between *humanitas* and
slavery is anything but timeless. Nevertheless I maintain that
our understanding has greater truth than, say, the understanding of classical antiquity. We may today be in the process of discovering new truths about the constitution and
scope of *humanitas* in the area of human rights. I think that
contemporary views on the equality of sexes (including the
"third sex" of so-called "erotic minorities") and of the races,
or on the "impossibility" of capital punishment, constitute
genuinely new discoveries of truths about man. At the same
time, it would almost certainly be an error to think of such
truths as "evolving" naturally or inevitably in the course of
history, or to think of history as a straight line of "progress,"
ascending of necessity to ever greater knowledge of the
truth about man. Truths can be discovered or rediscovered.
Truths can also be lost and forgotten again. History is not the
night in which all cats are gray, but neither is it a giant
escalator ascending to the point at which we happen to stand.
Each claim to truth must be looked at on its own merits—in
"immediacy to God," as the nineteenth-century historian
Ranke would have it—and simultaneously in full awareness

of its socio-historical location. Thus it is in no way certain, but altogether possible, that we know some things today about the scope of *humanitas* that have never been known before. It is also possible that there was a secret conclave of Aztec priests who knew something we have not even dreamed of—and that this truth perished with them, never to be recovered. A certain balance of brashness and modesty, in about equal measures, is a virtue when it comes to anthropological inquiry.

Let us return once more to the juxtaposition of the "natural" and the "supernatural," as these terms were used earlier. I maintain that there is a dichotomy in the human situation between a middle ground, which is the realm of ordinary, everyday life in society, and various marginal realms in which the taken-for-granted assumptions of the former realm are threatened or put in question. As Alfred Schutz has shown, the middle ground, which we take for granted as normality and sanity, can be maintained (that is, inhabited) only if we suspend all doubt about its validity. Without this suspension of doubt, everyday life would be impossible, if only because it would be constantly invaded by the "fundamental anxiety" caused by our knowledge and fear of death. This implies that all human societies and their institutions are, at their root, a barrier against naked terror.[43]

Nevertheless most historical societies have related the marginal experiences to those of the middle ground in a variety of ways, both practical and theoretical. There have been rituals to assuage, but at the same time to represent, the terror of the margins. Funeral rites or ceremonies regarding sexuality are examples of this. There have been theories that served to integrate the same margins with what Schutz called the "paramount reality" of everyday life, but that in doing so took cognizance of the reality of marginal experience. In other words, most historical societies have remained open to the metaphysical. Human life has always had a day-side and a night-side, and, inevitably, because of the practical requirements of man's being in the world, it has always been the day-side that has received the strongest "accent of reality." But the night-side, even if exorcised, was rarely denied. One of the most astonishing consequences of secularization has been just this denial. Modern society has banished the night from consciousness, as far as this is possible. The treatment of death in modern society, especially in America, is the sharpest manifestation of this.[44] Much more generally, modern society has not only sealed up the old metaphysical questions in practice, but (especially in the Anglo-Saxon countries) has generated philosophical positions that deny the meaningfulness of these questions. "What is the purpose of my life?" "Why must I die?" "Where do I come from and where will I go?" "Who am I?"—all such questions are not only suppressed in practice, but are theoretically liquidated by relegating them to meaninglessness. To repeat a simile used before, the reality of a middle-aged businessman drowsily digesting his lunch is elevated to the status of final philosophical authority. All questions that do not correspond to this reality are ruled to be inadmissible. The denial of metaphysics may here be identified with the triumph of triviality.

How long such a shrinkage in the scope of human experience can remain plausible is debatable. In any case, it constitutes a profound impoverishment. Both in practice and in theoretical thought, human life gains the greatest part of its richness from the capacity for ecstasy, by which I do not mean the alleged experiences of the mystic, but any experience of stepping outside the taken-for-granted reality of everyday life, any openness to the mystery that surrounds us on all sides. A philosophical anthropology worthy of the name will have to regain a perception of these experiences, and with this regain a metaphysical dimension. The theological method suggested here as a possibility will contribute to this rediscovery of ecstasy and metaphysics as crucial dimensions of human life, and by the same token to the recovery of lost riches of both experience and thought.

4. Theological Possibilities: Confronting the Traditions

It should be amply clear by now that, however it may have appeared in some early sections of this book, I am *not* proposing a theological program of conservative restoration. My repudiation of the trivialities of recent "radical" theology, and of the secularized consciousness that this theology seeks to legitimate, is not an invitation to seek refuge in the firm (*sic*) fortresses of tradition. The terms I have used to outline a possible theological method—"anthropological starting point," "empirically given," and "inductive faith"—are intrinsically repulsive to most conservative forms of theology. Their natural affinity is with theological liberalism, especially that movement of Protestant liberal theology that began with Schleiermacher and, as I have suggested, was only temporarily interrupted by the neo-orthodox reaction following World War I.

Indeed, it is perhaps two different understandings of the *relationship* between faith and reason that constitute the crucial division between conservative and liberal modes of theologizing. It is most inaccurate to reproach all conservative theology with irrationality or all liberal theology with timidity of faith. The issue lies, rather, in the manner in which two movements of the mind are related. Conservative theology, however rational it may be in its method, tends to *deduce* from the tradition. Liberal theology, however much it may emphasize the necessity of faith, tends to *induce* from generally accessible experience. It would be puerile to make moral or psychological judgments on this difference. Let me simply emphasize once more my conviction that it is the method of "inductive faith" that holds the greatest promise of new approaches to religious truth in an intellectual situation marked by a pervasive sense of relativity.

The problem of making faith plausible is not new. It was Augustine who formulated it with the sharpest accuracy when he said: *"Nullus quippe credit aliquid, nisi prius cogitaverit esse credendum"*—"No one, indeed, believes anything, unless he previously knows it to be believable."[45] The only edge we may conceivably have today over Augustine in this insight is a more systematic awareness of the social dynamics of both *cogitatio* and *credenda*, of what is known and what is believed—an awareness that I discussed in terms of the sociology of knowledge in the section on plausibility structures. This new awareness, however, greatly increases the difficulty of simply submitting to tradition, and thus tends toward inductive modes of theological thought.

The theological method I have suggested here is strongly inclined toward an independent stance vis-à-vis the various religious traditions. But the problem of confronting the traditions remains, and no theological method is likely to be very productive unless it seriously faces this problem. Why? It is perhaps more useful to say why *not*. From the point of view presented in this book, the traditions must *not* be confronted because they have some mysterious but irresistible claim to our loyalty. Such notions have a curious persistence, even among intellectuals who have largely emancipated themselves from their respective religious backgrounds, but who nevertheless view the respective traditions as somehow part of the individual's being—an inner reality that he must confront. In the Western world, such an attitude is most frequently found among Jews, for historically understandable reasons. But among Christians, too, we come across such statements as "I must find out more about my faith," or, even more sharply, "I really ought to learn what we believe." The terms "faith" and "we" refer, of course, to the religious community from which the individual happens to come. Putting the matter this way illuminates the weakness in logic of the underlying attitude, whatever its *psychological* plausibility. Faith, in the proper meaning of the word, is or is not held. If it is, no "learning" is necessary; if it is not, one cannot refer to it as one's own. And the "we" of a religious community, which is by definition based on a religious faith held in common, cannot be logically taken as anteceding that faith except, perhaps, as a sociological proposition—but that is not what people who speak this way mean.

One can, of course, understand and sympathize with this attitude; there are often obvious, psychological reasons why people feel this way. There is even something touching about a Jewish agnostic who feels twitches of conscience as he eats his dinner on Yom Kippur, or a skeptic of Catholic antecedents who senses a pressure under his kneecaps as the host is carried by on Corpus Christi. If such psychological data are elevated to become criteria of truth, however, they become mystifications that perform the function Sartre called "bad faith"—that is, they misrepresent choice as destiny and thus deny the choices actually made. To be sure, such ideas as the eternal efficacy of "Jewish blood" or of the sacrament of baptism do much to give Jewishness or Christianity "indelible character." Once a Jew, always a Jew. Once baptized, forever a Christian. Ideas of this sort are, I think, essentially magical. Within the frame of reference suggested here, they must be interpreted as dehumanizing distortions of the empirical reality of our existence.

There are better reasons why the traditions must be confronted. On the most obvious level, the adage that "he who ignores history is condemned to repeat it" holds for the theologian as well. The fundamental questions of theology have been passionately considered for at least three thousand years. It is not only insufferable arrogance to think that one can begin theologizing in sovereign disregard of this history; it is also extremely uneconomical. It seems rather a waste of time to spend, say, five years working out a position, only to find that it has already been done by a Syrian monk in the fifth century. The very least that a knowledge of religious traditions has to offer is a catalogue of heresies for possible home use.

More importantly, though, the method I have been suggesting precludes turning away from history. If human experience contains theologically relevant data, the historical dimension of all human experience must be taken into account theologically. If there are genuine cases of the discovery of religious truth, we must come to grips with their history, for the very word "discovery" implies a historical process. This is even more clearly the case if we repudiate the idea of "progress." If all history were a steady progression, there might be a certain logic to ignoring the past. By definition, every past situation would in its approach to truth be inferior to the present. One would concern oneself with the past, if at all, simply for self-satisfied edification, in about the same mood as that of some early ethnologists' studies of "savages." But if, on the other hand, each age is seen in its "immediacy to God," each age must be carefully looked at for whatever signals of transcendence might be uniquely its own. To return to an earlier example, the theologian must concern himself with history because there is at least the possibility of his finding out about that one, never-to-be-repeated flash of truth which was the secret possession of a cabal of Aztec priests—and which might, who knows, provide the solution to his own most pressing problem.

By the same logic, this confrontation with the past cannot be limited to any one tradition, however much an individual may be personally attached to it. Theologizing today must take place in an ecumenical consciousness. In our present, pluralistic situation, it is becoming more and more difficult to stay religiously *entre nous*. All religious groups are constantly confronted by the massive presence of a secularized world view in its multiform manifestations and, on top of that, keep bumping into each other at every turn. Christian bumps into Jew, Catholic into Protestant, while the intra-Protestant bumping process has attained almost orgiastic intensity. With a little bit of luck one may even bump into the latest jet-propelled guru, fresh from the East with religious luggage of appropriately light weight for convenient air travel. Today everyone is forced into a permanent conversation with everyone else, which is mostly carried on in a very polite manner. It is funny, but, I daresay, it is also salutary. It is healthy for nuns to have to deal with rabbis, and vice versa, and it won't hurt either group to come up against a few Hindu holy men. In any case it is very difficult to ignore ecumenical consciousness, even if one desires to.

In this particular instance, the practical necessity is tantamount to a theoretical blessing. For an ecumenical consciousness makes possible a mode of theologizing that is very aware of the fullness of man's religious quest in a way that is probably unparalleled in the history of religion. It thus increases the likelihood that no genuine discovery of religious truth will be overlooked simply because of the accident of the theologian's birth.

The actual pressures of the pluralistic situation are further augmented by the unprecedented availability of the past as a result of modern historical scholarship. The contemporary theologian has within his reach an incredible wealth of information about man's religious thought in every known period of history—often in the form of inexpensive paperbacks! It is hard to see how intelligent use of this opportunity can fail to redound to the benefit of the theological enterprise. There is no longer any excuse for theological ethnocentrism.

It should today be inconceivable to carry on theological work without taking cognizance of this ecumenical abundance. Within the camp of Western Christianity, at least, this is coming to be generally accepted, and the ecumenical movement properly speaking has tried to bring Eastern Christianity more and more into the "polylogue" (if the term will be permitted). In America the conversation between Christianity and Judaism, too, has increasingly come to be regarded as a desirable exercise. But however much all this is to be welcomed, it is still too narrow a definition of ecumenical consciousness. After all, Christians and Jews are in the position of first cousins talking to each other. At the very least, they ought to draw into the conversation their second cousins from the House of Islam. And it is very much to be wished (and very probably inevitable) that the conversation be extended to include the great religious traditions of India and the Far East, both as they presently exist and as they are available in the respective literatures. It should not be necessary to belabor the point that this desideratum is implied in the particular method I have suggested.

Ecumenical consciousness should be more than a response to practical necessities or an accommodation to intercultural good manners as practiced in the United Nations delegates'

lounge. It is not a question of becoming sophisticated about
or polite to people who, say, worship cows or are worried
about swatting flies. It is a question of seriously attempting
an inductive approach to the theological enterprise. One
point should, however, be strongly emphasized. I am *not* rec-
ommending the construction of a catchall system, a sort of
theological Esperanto in which all traditions will be dissolved.
On the contrary, ecumenical consciousness should be particularly conducive to the clarification of contradictory options. Only when these options have become fully conscious
will it be possible to understand them as *available choices*.
In other words, only an ecumenically conscious theology is
in the position of really being able to make choices—be they
choices between historically available traditions, or choices
that modify these traditions, or perhaps a choice to strike out
in new directions in opposition to all the traditions. For example, any attempt to blend Christianity and Buddhism is
almost certainly based on ignorance of one or both of these
traditions. Christianity and Buddhism present us with clear
and, I think, essentially contradictory religious options. The
protagonists of both religions should be clear about what
both options are, and so should the people who choose neither
religion. Almost inevitably, the knowledge of these historical
options will enrich the intellectual clarity of the individual's
own choice.

These ideas are by no means new. They were very common
during the heyday of Protestant theological liberalism and
were a powerful factor in the growth of the historical and
comparative study of religion during the same period. There
was at the time a very strong expectation in scholarly circles
and among laymen that this kind of engagement with the
wealth of man's religious quest, past and present, would en-
able men to make more rational choices in this area. One
may recall here by way of examples the immense effort that
went into Max Müller's compilation of the *Sacred Books of
the East* and, on the popular side, the excitement generated
in the 1890s by the World Parliament of Religions, held in
conjunction with the Chicago World's Fair. The scholarly
achievements of this era are monumental and even today
form the indispensable foundation for almost all work in the

history of religion. But we would do well not to be too blasé about the less scholarly manifestations of this "premature ecumenism." I am not suggesting that one should be terribly impressed by little old ladies in tennis shoes rushing about to proclaim "*Ex oriente lux*" with a Midwestern accent (though, I confess, I find them considerably more impressive than intellectuals of any accent who are convinced that no light can come from anywhere outside their own depressing cliques). But even this kind of popularizing activity (I mean, of course, the little old ladies, not the intellectuals' cliques) can serve as an important part of the plausibility structure of an intellectually more serious enterprise.

I am not, as I stressed earlier, suggesting a simple return to an earlier period of religious thought either. In religion as in anything else it is almost never possible to return to an earlier state of affairs. Nor would I want to. I certainly would not want to revive the shallow faith in progress, the dreary rationalism, or the smug self-satisfaction of the *belle époque*, even if it were feasible. But, to repeat, I *would* want to revive a deeper motif of what has justly been called the Schleiermacher era—a spirit of patient induction and an attitude of openness to the fullness of human experience, especially as this experience is accessible to historical inquiry.

The traditions, *all* the traditions, must be confronted in search of whatever signals of transcendence may have been sedimented in them. This means an approach grounded in empirical methods of inquiry (most importantly, of course, in the methods of modern historical scholarship) and free of dogmatic a prioris (free, that is, of the dogmatic assumptions of the neo-orthodox reaction). A few years ago a group of younger Protestant theologians in Germany published a collective work, intended as a sharp challenge to neo-orthodoxy and provocatively entitled *Revelation as History*.[46] The key figure in this group is Wolfhart Pannenberg, whose work continues to emphasize both empirical history and empirical anthropology. I strongly endorse this approach. But I would prefer an emphasis on "discovery" as against "revelation." To be sure, if one has already achieved faith, one will see any manifestation of transcendence as a revelation or, as Mircea Eliade puts it, a "theophany." But it is precisely this "already achieved" status that I would like to get away from in terms of theological method, at least in its starting point. To speak of "revelation" before one is sure just where one may speak of "discovery" is putting the cart before the horse.[47]

History provides us with the record of man's experience with himself and with reality. This record contains those experiences, in a variety of forms, that I have called signals of transcendence. The theological enterprise will have to be first of all, a rigorously empirical analysis of these experiences, in terms of both a historical anthropology and a history of religion, and, if my suggestion is followed, the former will have logical priority over the latter. The theological enterprise will go beyond the empirical frame of reference at the point where it begins to speak of discoveries and to explicate what is deemed to have been discovered—that is, at the point where the transcendent intentions in human experience are treated as *realities* rather than as *alleged realities*.

Needless to say, this transition from empirical analysis to metaphysics is in itself an act of faith. Only in the anticipation of such faith will theology separate itself from the empirical study of man and his religious productions. And only then will it become theology in the etymologically proper sense of the word. Thus it is absurd to speak of a "scientific theology" (as, for example, has been the tendency in Scandinavia, particularly in Sweden, where theology has been virtually absorbed in the phenomenology and history of religion). In any empirical frame of reference, transcendence must appear as a projection of man. Therefore, if transcendence is to be spoken of *as* transcendence, the empirical frame of reference must be left behind. It cannot be otherwise. My concern is the method by which this switch in frames of reference is to be attained.

An example may make this clearer. Much has been made in recent Protestant theology of the centralness of Christ and the alleged necessity of starting the theological enterprise with the figure of Christ. At its worst, this approach systematizes the rape of the historical materials, as when Christian beliefs are read back into the religious history of ancient Israel. But even at its most sophisticated, when history is treated carefully and respectfully, it means that all theological interpretations of historical materials should emanate from this one central focus, which is itself taken as an unchanging a priori. I repudiate such a procedure. I would take the historical materials concerning Christ, both the New Testament itself and the subsequent literature, as a record of a specific complex of human experience. As such, it has no special position as against any comparable record (say, the record concerning the Buddha in the Pali canon and the subsequent ramifications of Buddhist thought). The questions I would then ask would be essentially the same as on any other record: *What is being said here? What is the human experience out of which these statements come?* And then: *To what extent, and in what way, may we see here genuine discoveries of transcendent truth?*

I must leave aside the question whether, in this particular instance, this approach calls for a renewal of the "quest for the historical Jesus," as some New Testament scholars have recently urged, or whether we must remain satisfied with the position of the Bultmann school that the historical Jesus remains inaccessible and that, willy-nilly, we are stuck with the Christ proclaimed as divine savior by the early church. This question exceeds both my scope and my competence. It is the methodological question that interests me here. I would go back to the classical *modus operandi* of nineteenth-century biblical scholarship. I would also go back to the spirit of relentless honesty, which is not so much disrespectful of established religious authority as ruthless with one's own religious hopes. Protestantism, the first religious tradition that found the courage to turn the sharp instruments of empirical inquiry back upon itself, has good reason to be proud of this spirit. In this sense (and not in the sense of an a priori commitment to a particular tradition) the procedure I am suggesting partakes of the "living, moving restless power" of what Paul Tillich called "the Protestant principle": "Protestantism has a principle that stands beyond all its realizations. . . . The Protestant principle is the judge of every religious and cultural reality, including the religion and culture which calls itself 'Protestant.' "[48] In this sense, and in this sense only, the approach I would take to the phenomenon of Christ is unabashedly Protestant. The "judgment" that is implied in this approach is as far as can be from self-satisfied arrogance in the face of the religious ecstasies of man. On the contrary, it is animated by patient openness and humility before all available intimations of religious truth.

I have in this chapter emphasized the necessity for the theological enterprise to confront the religious traditions, both those of the theologian's own cultural and biographical background and those that are foreign to it. I hope I have made clear that this does not contradict what I said in the preceding chapter about an anthropological starting point for theology. I am not now substituting historical scholarship for anthropology in the recommended starting point. I am, however, suggesting that the theological enterprise ought to entail confrontations of more than one kind. In addition to the confrontation with what can be empirically discovered about man and his works (which will be, above all, a confrontation with philosophical anthropology and with the socio-historical sciences of man), there must also be the confrontation with the contents of all the religious traditions both within and beyond one's own cultural milieu. There may also be the need to confront insights into man's reality from yet other sources, such as those the artist and the poet draw from. The search for signals of transcendence within human experience will hardly be able to afford to overlook such data as derive from, for instance, the creations of Bach or Mozart, of Gothic cathedral builders, or of Chagall, Hölderlin, or Blake (to mention names at random). As yet, we can barely conceive of the procedures by which this particular confrontation might be realized.

It is hardly staggering news to suggest that theology should engage in a many-sided conversation with other intellectual disciplines, certainly not in a situation in which the word "dialogue" has become a fashionable cliché. Nor would the substitution of the term "polylogue" be a worthwhile improvement. Everything, however, depends upon the manner in which this many-sided conversation is carried on, and a good deal will depend on the motives with which it is entered. There is no need to reiterate my earlier strictures on the motives of "with-it-ness" and of gaining the attention of the latest coterie of "cultured despisers of religion" to be picked up by the mass media. Any motive other than the search for truth degrades theology, as it degrades any other intellectual enterprise. Even the motive of pastoral or evangelistic concern is no exception to this. But the manner of confrontation is of decisive importance. "Dialogue" can be an alibi for charlatanism, in which everybody talks to everybody and nobody has anything to say. The so-called dynamics of communication can never be a substitute for the hard labor of intellectual effort. But "dialogue" can also be an inner necessity of a particular intellectual situation. Then it is undertaken with no other motive except the search for truth and not as a putative short cut to insights that can be obtained only by rigorous application. This I would welcome as one of the most promising possibilities of our contemporary situation. I also think that theologizing in this attitude can be one of the most exciting intellectual activities in this situation.

At the same time it must be recognized that religion is not primarily an activity of intellectuals, indeed cannot be understood as a primarily theoretical endeavor. The fundamental religious impulse is not to theorize about transcendence but to worship it. This is so regardless of whether religion animates large numbers of people in a society or is limited to what I have called cognitive minorities. If religion in our situation could manifest itself only as a theoretical concern, however passionate, of segments of the intelligentsia, this would in itself be a symptom of its progressive or impending demise. Any such intellectualism is particularly repugnant to the Judaeo-Christian traditions, in which faith has always been understood in relation to the actual life, work, and hope of human communities that include ditchdiggers as well as theoreticians. I therefore recognize that the theological enterprise I am speaking of, even if it employs the most complex tools of the intellectual's trade, will always push toward expression in living communities of men other than intellectuals. It would be foolhardy to speculate on the social forms that such communities might eventually take. But it is possible to extend the concept of pluralism to such communities. Some of them may well emerge within the traditional religious groupings or institutions, as new variants of the classical type of the *ecclesiola in ecclesia* (the "little church within the church," as a more intimate grouping within the larger community). There are already indications of this possibility in a variety of groups that (probably mis-leadingly) have been subsumed under the phrase "under-ground churches." Other such communities may congeal outside the lines drawn in our society by the religious institu-tions, outside the gates of the churches and possibly with little or no connection with the latter's traditional contents. Examples of this already exist too. Whether these communi-ties tend toward "sectarian" or "churchly" (or, in the Ameri-can context, "denominational") social forms will depend, as we have seen, upon the degree to which their contents deviate from the cognitive consensus of the over-all society. In either eventuality, as long as the religious contents are "living" rather than "dead," the communities embodying them will be communities of practice as well as theory. The practice may take different forms (conceivably political forms as well), but one form that will inevitably reappear, because of the intrinsic nature of man's religion, is worship. It is in worship that the prototypical gesture of religion is realized again and again. This is the gesture in which man reaches out in hope toward transcendence.

Unavoidably both this chapter and the preceding one have turned out to contain programs. Under ideal circumstances I would have had to wait until, say, the tenth anniversary of my retirement before I would have been in a position to present even a rough design of these programs. I must confess to a rather American lack of patience with such intellectual asceticism. But I must also confess to being very susceptible to another American propensity, to wit, the feeling that peo-ple should put up or shut up. Being unwilling (evidently) to shut up, and being unable to put up to the desired degree, I would still like to venture a few steps beyond program-making. Just as I earlier attempted to indicate what an an-thropological starting point for theology might mean, so I ought properly to conclude this chapter with at least some indications of how the traditions might be confronted in terms of the theological program I have suggested. For obvious reasons of economy, these remarks will be limited to the Christian tradition.[49]

One possibility would be a differentiated approach to the tradition. With regard to some elements of the tradition I can see a strong reaffirmation of their classical formulations, a reaffirmation *adversus modernos*, "against the moderns," in the teeth of secularized consciousness. With regard to other elements, I can see only the possibility of extracting certain discoveries from their classical context and starting anew the task of theological formulation. My approach would thus be "heretical" in the strict sense of the word—a theological stance marked by selectivity vis-à-vis the tradition. I will leave it to others to assign my selections to this or that entry in the voluminous catalogue of ancient heresies that every dogmatician seems to carry around in his head. Apart from the pleasure of recognition that may be obtained from stumbling upon ideological buddies in, say, ancient Alexandria or Antioch, such assignments can be of serious significance only to the orthodox.

Adversus modernos, I would, above all, reaffirm the conception of God that emerged in the religious experience of ancient Israel and that is available to us in the literature of the Old Testament. It is possible, with all deliberation and with full awareness of the immense cross-cultural range of human religion, to speak here of *a discovery of God*. The God whom Israel discovered (in its own self-understanding, of course, it was this God who revealed Himself to Israel) was an unheard-of novelty in the context of the religious world of the ancient Near East. He was the God who was wholly other with regard to the "natural" reality of human experience, not to be found either within man (as in the orgiastic religions of the surrounding cultures) or within the world (as in any conception of a necessary connection between a divinity and a particular people). He stood outside man and outside the world, yet He was also the creator of both man and world. His sovereign transcendence and otherness did not, however, imply indifference or inaccessibility to the reality of human experience. On the contrary, this God is encountered as a God who speaks to man and whose manifestations are to be sought, above all, in the historical events

of human experience. And God's speaking to man takes, first
and foremost, the form of an overpowering ethical demand.

In its central conception of God the biblical tradition (in
which, in this respect, we ought to include not only Judaism
and Christianity, but most definitely also Islam, with its violent protest against any dilutions of the transcendent majesty
of God) is set off sharply against the great religious traditions of India and the Far East, and also against the this-
worldliness and neo-mysticism of modern Western secular-
ism, which, whenever it becomes restless in its prison house,
can look for an escape only in one or another expedition into
the alleged depths of human consciousness itself (as in the
various forms of contemporary psychological salvation). Mysticism, broadly speaking, is any religious practice or doctrine
that asserts the ultimate unity of man and the divine. This
fundamental quality of mysticism has been classically formulated in Hinduism by the formula *tat tvam asi*—"thou art
that," that is, the depths of the human soul are identical
with the divine depths of the universe. Mystical religion,
therefore, always looks for salvation within the putative
depths of human consciousness itself. This is why the term
"neo-mysticism" fits much of what goes on today under the
banner of psychotherapy. All these quests for salvation from
within are diametrically opposed to the biblical conception
of God as one standing outside and against man.

The God of the biblical tradition is the polar antithesis of
the great identity proclaimed by the mystics, and of any possible variation on this theme. To reaffirm this discovery of
God in our situation might necessitate the formulation of
new creeds, though their content would in this case be quite
traditional—the reaffirmation of God who is not the world
and who was not made by man, who is outside and not within
ourselves, who is not a sign of human things but of whom
human things are signs, who is symbolized and not a symbol.
It is *this* God, totally other and yet accessible in human experience, in whom faith will see the foundation of order,
justice, and compassion in the world. It is *this* transcendence
of which certain human gestures in the world are signals. And
it is the faith in *this* God that (as it did in the religious his-

tory of Israel) eventuates in a hope that reaches beyond the confines of death.

These affirmations are Jewish or Muslim as much as they are Christian. In terms of the classical Christian creeds, they refer to the first rather than the second or third article of faith. It is with respect to these latter strata in the tradition that I would find a new theological venture more plausible than a reformation of traditional orthodoxies. If one can, indeed, speak of a discovery of Christ as one can of a discovery of God, then I see the link between the two in the agonizing problem of theodicy. All Christology is concerned with salvation. To speak of Christ is to speak of man's redemption, even in the seemingly most abstruse Christological controversies. For instance, some modern commentators have been amused by the violent debates in the early church as to whether God and Christ are to be understood as *homoiousion* ("of similar substance") or as *homoousion* ("of the same substance")—all this commotion over one letter! But in this one Greek letter *iota* rested the whole question of how Christ could be the hope for man's salvation. The *homoousion* formula was finally accepted by the church, not because of some esoteric philosophical logic, but because it was necessary to faith to affirm that it was God, and truly God, who was incarnate in Christ, suffered, and rose again for man's salvation.

A quest for redemption is by no means the prerogative of the biblical tradition. One has only to recall the importance of the idea of *moksha* (release from the sorrows of existence) in the religious formulations of ancient India. And despite the vast differences in the conceptions of just what man is to be redeemed from and how this might be accomplished (as, say, between a biblical conception of man's sin and the Hindu view of man's predicament), there is a common, empirically given human reality that underlies all quests for redemption. This is the reality of suffering, of evil, and of death.

To be sure, there is an immense difference between Job's perplexity about his misfortune in the context of a belief in the omnipotence of God and the Buddha's reflection about the roots of human suffering in the context of a belief in the endless wheel of rebirths. But the empirical reality of suffering in ancient Israel and ancient India could not have been very different. The begging leper, who was one of the four sights that led the young Buddha to retire from the world and seek redemption, must have looked very much like that afflicted Israelite, covered "with loathsome sores from the sole of his foot to the crown of his head" (Job 2:7).

The agonizing question about the ultimate meaning of human suffering and evil is, however, immeasurably aggravated by the conception of God in the biblical tradition. The discovery of the one God, all-powerful and all-good, creator of the world and sovereign of history, had to raise the question of theodicy in its sharpest possible form. All Christology, I believe, is at root an answer to this question.

The discovery of Christ implies the discovery of the redeeming presence of God within the anguish of human experience. Now God is perceived not only in terrible confrontation with the world of man, but present within it as suffering love. This presence makes possible the ultimate vindication of the creation, and thus the reconciliation between the power and the goodness of the creator. By the same token, it vindicates the hope that human suffering has redeeming significance. The history of man comes to be seen as one vast movement toward the moment when this vindication will become manifest (in the language of the New Testament, when the Kingdom of God will have finally come). In Christ, however, this final vindication is anticipated. Redemption is yet to come, as the world "in this eon" is still dominated by suffering, evil, and death. But redemption is already present here and now because, hidden within the empirical reality of the world, the essential work of redemption has already been accomplished. This *presence* of redemption is accessible to faith here and now, not only in the hope for the coming consummation. It is this duality of anticipation and presentness that sets off Christian faith, on the one hand from the timeless ecstasy of all mysticism, on the other hand from the grim imprisonment in history of all this-worldly doctrines of salvation (notably the Marxist one).

To this extent, of course, such a Christological formulation is amenable to incorporation within this or that orthodox position. Where it becomes hopelessly heterodox is in its omission of the historical reference to that Jesus who was crucified under Pontius Pilate. It can hardly be doubted that it was in connection with the events surrounding the life of Jesus that this new understanding of God's relationship to man emerged. This is admitted by both those who want to root Christian faith in the historical figure and those who would see only the figure as witnessed to (and, presumably, transformed) in the message of the early church. However important may be the findings of historical scholarship on these events, I find it difficult to see how, in the wake of all the relativizations of which we must take cognizance today, an inductive faith can rest upon the exclusive authority of these events—and thus, how the discovery of Christ as the redeeming presence of God in the world can be exclusively linked to the figure of the historical Jesus. If *this* exclusiveness is to be identified with the much-vaunted historical character of Christian faith, then perhaps this particular historical character will have to be left behind in favor of a more ecumenical one. With this heterodox *haeresis*, however, the exclusiveness of the Christian tradition will be relativized in the second as well as the third article of faith (the articles about Christ and the church), as classically formulated.

I see Christ as historically manifested in Jesus but not historically given (as the splendidly defiant particularity of the creedal phrase "under Pontius Pilate" or the all too precise specificity of the dating of events surrounding the birth of Jesus in Luke 3:1-2 suggest). In other words, the redeeming presence of God in the world is manifested in history, but it is not given once and for all in the particular historical events reported on in the New Testament. I am then constrained to disregard the insistence of the New Testament authors that redemption lies only "in this name" of Jesus Christ (that is, the name that links the historical figure with the cosmic scope of God's redeeming presence). This leads on to the affirmation that while Christ can be and has been "named," He is not identical with any name—an affirmation close to those Christian heresies that de-emphasized the historical Jesus as against the cosmic Christ, redeemer of all possible worlds. But I would not wish to share in the turning from history and in the pessimism of many of these heresies (notably, of course, the Gnostic ones).

It follows that the community (or, more exactly, communities) in which Christ becomes manifest cannot be identified with any particular "names" or traditions, though He may be more manifest in some than in others. The presence of Christ will have to be determined not by a direct succession from a certain point in the past, but rather from such evidence as can be found in the empirical reality of communities whose actions can be called redemptive. Wherever communities gather around acts of redeeming love, there we may look for the presence of Christ. The redemptive community of Christ in the world must be seen as ever coming into being again in the empirical history of man. It will be there implicitly wherever the redeeming gestures of love, hope, and compassion are reiterated in human experience. It will become explicit wherever these gestures are understood in relation to the God who both created and redeems the world, who may well have been "in Jesus," but who is ever again present in the human imitations of redemptive love. Every such community, whether implicitly in its actions or explicitly in its worship, anticipates here and now the consummation of redemption toward which the world is moving.

I am well aware of the fact that, in the attempt to show how an inductive theological position might confront a particular religious tradition, I have swung wildly to right and left, cutting through a multitude of Gordian knots carefully tied together in centuries of theological cerebration. Each statement in the preceding paragraphs, to be properly defended (or, as the Germans so nicely put it, "protected"), would require a book at least as long as this one. I plead guilty to the charge of "terrible simplification." It could be, though, that a certain kind of simplification is long overdue in the business of theologizing. I hope that it is the simplification not of ignorance, but of an effort to get at basic questions. The point could also be made that many new intellectual departures have become possible only after the luxuriant complexities accumulated before them have once more been reduced to surveyable simplicity.

5. Concluding Remarks—
A Rumor of Angels

"Everything is full of gods," exclaimed Thales of Miletus. Biblical monotheism swept away the gods in the glorification of the awesome majesty of the One, but the fullness that overwhelmed Thales continued to live on for a long time in the figures of the angels, those beings of light who are witness to the fullness of the divine glory. In the prophetic visions they surround the throne of God. Again and again, in the pages of both the Old and New Testaments, they appear as messengers (*angeloi*) of this God, signalizing His transcendence as well as His presence in the world of man. Above all, angels signal God's concern for this world, both in judgment and in redemption. Nothing is left out of this concern. As a rabbinical writer put it, "There's not a stalk on earth that has not its (protecting or guardian) angel in heaven."[50] In the religious view of reality, all phenomena point toward that which transcends them, and this transcendence actively impinges from all sides on the empirical sphere of human existence.

It was only with the onset of secularization that the divine fullness began to recede, until the point was reached when the empirical sphere became both all-encompassing and perfectly closed in upon itself. At that point man was truly alone in reality. We have come a long way from the gods and from the angels. The breaches of this-worldly reality which these mighty figures embodied have increasingly vanished from our consciousness as serious possibilities. They linger on as fairy tales, nostalgias, perhaps as vague symbols of some sort. A few years ago, a priest working in a slum section of a European city was asked why he was doing it, and replied, "So that the rumor of God may not disappear completely." The word aptly expresses what the signals of transcendence have become in our situation—rumors—and not very reputable rumors at that.

This book has not been about angels. At best, it might be a preface to angelology, if by that one meant a study of God's messengers as His signals in reality. We are, whether we like it or not, in a situation in which transcendence has been reduced to a rumor. We cannot escape our situation with one magical jump. We cannot readily, and probably should not wish to, return to an earlier situation in the history of man's grappling with reality. For this reason I have taken pains, at a number of points in my argument, to stress that what I am advocating is neither esoteric nor "reactionary." But I have also tried to show that our situation is not an inexorable fate and that secularized consciousness is not the absolute it presents itself as. We must begin in the situation in which we find ourselves, but we must not submit to it as to an irresistible tyranny. If the signals of transcendence have become rumors in our time, then we can set out to explore these rumors—and perhaps to follow them up to their source.

A rediscovery of the supernatural will be, above all, a regaining of openness in our perception of reality. It will not only be, as theologians influenced by existentialism have greatly overemphasized, an overcoming of tragedy. Perhaps more importantly it will be an overcoming of triviality. In openness to the signals of transcendence the true proportions of our experience are rediscovered. This is the comic relief of redemption; it makes it possible for us to laugh and to play with a new fullness. This in no way implies a remoteness from the moral challenges of the moment, but rather the most careful attention to each human gesture that we encounter or that we may be called upon to perform in the everyday dramas of human life—literally, an "infinite care" in the affairs of men—just because, in the words of the New Testament writer, it is in the midst of these affairs that "some have entertained angels unawares." (Hebrews 13:2)

I think that the openness and the reproportioning this attitude entails have a moral significance, even a political significance, of no mean degree. The principal moral benefit of religion is that it permits a confrontation with the age in which one lives in a perspective that transcends the age and thus puts it in proportion. This both vindicates courage and safeguards against fanaticism. To find courage to do what must be done in a given moment is not the only moral good. It is also very much a moral good that this same moment does not become the be-all and end-all of one's existence, that in meeting its demands one does not lose the capacity to laugh and to play. One must have experienced the grim humorlessness of contemporary revolutionary ideologies to appreciate fully the humanizing power of the religious perspective. It is hardly necessary to insist here on the moral demands of our situation, especially in America today; they stagger the imagination. Whether we approach them in a mood of doomsday or of renewed hope in the efficacy of particular programs of action often depends on whether we have just read the morning or the afternoon paper. In either case one of the best things that can happen to us is to recall that, to use Dietrich Bonhoeffer's suggestive term, all historical events are "penultimate," that their ultimate significance lies in a reality that transcends them and that transcends all the empirical coordinates of human existence.

For most of this book I have discussed the rediscovery of the supernatural as a possibility for theological thought in our time. It is impossible to know for sure whether any such rediscovery will remain the property of more or less isolated cognitive minorities, or whether it may also have an impact of larger historical dimensions. It is possible to speculate, even to venture prognoses, on the basis of what is empirically knowable in the present, but all "futurology" is a tenuous business. The sociologist and probably any other empirical observer of human events will be tempted to prognosticate, and I too have yielded to the temptation earlier. But I would like to emphasize once more that anyone who approaches religion with an interest in its possible truth, rather than in this or that aspect of its social manifestations, would do well to cultivate a measure of indifference in the matter of empirical prognoses. History brings out certain questions of truth, makes certain answers more or less accessible, constructs and disintegrates plausibility structures. But the historical course of the question about transcendence cannot, of itself, answer the question. It is only human to be exhilarated if one thinks one is riding on the crest of the future. All too often, however, such exhilaration gives way to the sobering recognition that what looked like a mighty wave of history was only a marginal eddy in the stream of events. For the theologian, if not for the social scientist, I would therefore suggest a moratorium on the anxious query as to just who it is that has modernity by the short hair. Theology must begin and end with the question of truth. My concern here has been with some possible methods of pursuing this question today.

Notes

1. Thomas J. J. Altizer and William Hamilton, *Radical Theology and the Death of God* (Indianapolis, Bobbs-Merrill, 1966), p. 11.
2. Herman Kahn and Anthony J. Wiener, *The Year 2000—A Framework for Speculation on the Next Thirty-three Years* (New York, Macmillan, 1967), p. 7 (Table I).
3. Alfred Schutz, *Collected Papers* (The Hague, Nijhoff, 1962), vol. I, p. 208.
4. Thomas Luckmann, *The Invisible Religion—The Problem of Religion in Modern Society* (New York, Macmillan, 1967).
5. Most of these studies are not available in English. However, cf. the English-language journal of this group, *Social Compass*, published in Europe, as well as the American Catholic journal *Sociological Analysis*. Also, cf. the very useful reference work edited by Hervé Carrier and Emile Pin, *Sociology of Christianity—An International Bibliography* (Rome, Gregorian University Press, 1964). For the flavor of this approach, cf. the contributions of F. Boulard, F.-A. Isambert and Emile Pin in the reader edited by Louis Schneider, *Religion, Culture and Society* (New York, Wiley, 1964), pp. 385ff., 400ff., and 411ff.
6. Cf. Charles Glock and Rodney Stark, *Religion and Society in Tension* (Chicago, Rand McNally, 1965); N. J. Demerath II, *Social Class in American Protestantism* (Chicago, Rand McNally, 1965); Charles Glock, Benjamin Ringer and Earl Babbie, *To Comfort and to Challenge—A Dilemma of the Contemporary Church* (Berkeley, University of California Press, 1967). The most

important recent sociological study of American religion is still Gerhard Lenski, *The Religious Factor* (Garden City, N.Y., Doubleday, 1961).

7. For a systematic presentation of this, in terms of the sociology of knowledge, cf. Peter Berger and Thomas Luckmann, *The Social Construction of Reality* (Garden City, N.Y., Doubleday, 1966).

8. Cf. ibid., pp. 135ff. On the social-psychological processes involved in this, cf. Solomon Asch, *Social Psychology* (New York, Prentice-Hall, 1952), pp. 387ff.

9. Walter Kaufmann, *Nietzsche* (New York, Meridian Books, 1956), p. 81.

10. Cf. my "A Sociological View of the Secularization of Theology," *Journal for the Scientific Study of Religion*, Spring 1967, for a more detailed analysis of this constellation.

11. In a recent (unpublished) radio talk, "Sociologist Fallen Among Secular Theologians."

12. For a discussion of the religious dilemma of contemporary Judaism, cf. Arthur Cohen, *The Natural and the Supernatural Jew—A History and Theological Introduction* (New York, Pantheon Books, 1962).

13. Cf. Peter Berger and Thomas Luckmann, "Secularization and Pluralism," *International Yearbook for the Sociology of Religion*, 1966.

14. Cf. my *The Sacred Canopy—Elements of a Sociological Theory of Religion* (Garden City, N.Y., Doubleday, 1967), pp. 105ff.

15. On the contemporary religious market, cf. Berger and Luckmann, "Secularization and Pluralism," loc. cit.

16. Cf. Louis Pauwels and Jacques Bergier, *The Morning of the Magicians* (New York, Stein and Day, 1964).

17. Rose Goldsen et al., *What College Students Think* (Princeton, N.J., Nostrand, 1960).

18. Poll conducted on behalf of the news magazine *Der Spiegel* (21:52, December 18, 1967).

19. David Martin, *A Sociology of English Religion* (New York, Basic Books, 1967), p. 75.

20. Cf. John Petrie (ed.), *The Worker Priests—A Collective*

Documentation (London, Routledge and Kegan Paul, 1956).

21. Cf. Ernest Campbell and Thomas Pettigrew, *Christians in Racial Crisis—A Study of Little Rock's Ministry* (Washington, Public Affairs Press, 1959).

22. Cf. Berger and Luckmann, *Social Construction of Reality*, especially pp. 85ff., and my *Sacred Canopy*, especially pp. 126ff.

23. I made this distinction myself in an earlier discussion of some of these questions, *The Precarious Vision* (Garden City, N.Y., Doubleday, 1961); I must now disavow this approach.

24. Ludwig Feuerbach, *The Essence of Christianity* (New York, Harper, 1957), pp. xff.

25. Again, cf. Berger and Luckmann, "Secularization and Pluralism," loc. cit. Some of the social-psychological aspects of this interpretation of pluralism are derived from the work of the contemporary German sociologists Arnold Gehlen and Helmut Schelsky.

26. For a systematic development of this, again cf. my *Sacred Canopy*.

27. There is, of course, a vast literature on these theological developments, but one of the most useful analyses in English is still H. R. Mackintosh, *Types of Modern Theology*. Of the standard works in German, I have found Horst Stephan and Martin Schmidt, *Geschichte der deutschen evangelischen Theologie* very useful.

28. Albert Camus, *The Plague* (New York, Knopf, 1948), p. 278.

29. Again cf. my *Sacred Canopy*, especially cc. 1–2.

30. Eric Voegelin, *Order and History* (Baton Rouge, Louisiana State University Press, 1956), vol. I ("Israel and Revelation"), p. ix.

31. Cf. Johan Huizinga, *Homo Ludens—A Study of the Play Element in Culture* (Boston, Beacon Press, 1955).

32. On this cf. Schutz, op. cit.

33. *"Alle Lust will Ewigkeit—will tiefe, tiefe Ewigkeit!"*—Friedrich Nietzsche, *Also sprach Zarathustra* (Leipzig, Kroener, 1917), p. 333.

34. C. S. Lewis, *The Weight of Glory* (Grand Rapids, Mich., Eerdmans, 1965), pp. 44f.

35. Among Catholics by Karl Rahner, among Protestants by Jürgen Moltmann and Wolfhart Pannenberg.

36. These theological developments are very important, not only because of the specific attention they give to the phenomenon of hope, but because they take seriously the possibility of an anthropological starting point for theology. It seems to me, however, that the emphasis on hope as *the* theologically relevant anthropological element is far too narrow. This can probably be accounted for by two circumstances—among Protestants, the interest in affirming, against neo-orthodoxy, the empirical historicity of the Christian religion (which is then related to hope as an essential mode of the "futurity" of man)—among both Protestants and Catholics, the elaboration of these ideas in the dialogue with Marxism (in which Christian hope is set off against Marxist eschatology). I share the animus against the neo-orthodox treatment of empirical history as well as the concern for a dialogue with Marxism, but would still insist on a much broader anthropological focus.

37. Philip Rieff, *Freud—The Mind of the Moralist* (Garden City, N.Y., Doubleday-Anchor, 1961), pp. 329ff.

38. An earlier version of this argument may be found in my *Precarious Vision*, pp. 209ff. I have not changed my mind about this and what I say here is substantially a repetition.

39. Sigmund Freud, "Wit and Its Relation to the Unconscious," in A. A. Brill (ed.), *The Basic Writings of Sigmund Freud* (New York, Modern Library, 1938): Henri Bergson, "Laughter," in W. Sypher (ed.), *Comedy* (Garden City, N.Y., Doubleday-Anchor, 1956).

40. Bergson, op. cit., p. 123.

41. Alfred Schutz, "Don Quixote and the Problem of Reality," in *Collected Papers* (The Hague, Nijhoff, 1964), vol. II, p. 157.

42. Enid Welsford, *The Fool* (Garden City, N.Y., Doubleday-Anchor, 1961), pp. 326f.

43. This idea is developed systematically in *Sacred Canopy*, cc. 1–2.
44. Cf. Geoffrey Gorer, *Death, Grief and Mourning* (Garden City, N.Y., Doubleday, 1965). A good summation of the sociological import of this is a recent article by Philippe Ariès, *European Journal of Sociology*, 1967:2. Also cf. Barney Glaser and Anselm Strauss, *Awareness of Dying* (Chicago, Aldine, 1965), for an empirical study of this in a hospital setting.
45. *De praedestinatione sanctorum*, 2:5.
46. Wolfhart Pannenberg et al., *Offenbarung als Geschichte* (Göttingen, Vandenhöck & Ruprecht, 1963). The work has recently come out in an English version.
47. As far as I understand him, Pannenberg seems to be in accord with this idea. My remarks here are not intended as criticism of Pannenberg, but rather as a *caveat* against the premature "correlations" to which theologians with a biographical and existential standpoint within a particular tradition are understandably prone.
48. Paul Tillich, *The Protestant Era* (Chicago, University of Chicago Press, 1948), p. 163.
49. The following remarks, of course, contain allusions to a variety of theological positions and controversies. The theologically informed reader will readily identify these (and, more likely than not, deplore their application!). I have felt, though, that nothing would be gained by studding these paragraphs with references, which would only detract from consideration of the possibilities or impossibility of such an approach.
50. Cited in Gustav Davidson, *A Dictionary of Angels* (New York, Free Press, 1967), p. xv.

28E